BEST OF Aleene's Creative Living®

Oxmoor House®

Best of Aleene's Creative Living

Book Division of Southern Progress Corporation
P.O. Box 2463, Birmingham, Alabama 35201

Published by Oxmoor House, Inc., and Leisure Arts, Inc.

Library of Congress Catalog Card Number: 97-65762
Hardcover ISBN: 0-8487-1570-5
Softcover ISBN: 0-8487-1614-0
Manufactured in the United States of America
First Printing 1997

Editor-in-Chief: Nancy Fitzpatrick Wyatt
Senior Crafts Editor: Susan Ramey Cleveland
Senior Editor, Editorial Services: Olivia Kindig Wells
Art Director: James Boone

Best of Aleene's Creative Living
Editor: Margaret Allen Price
Editorial Assistant: Barzella Estle
Copy Editor: Susan S. Cheatham
Designer: Carol Damsky
Illustrator: Kelly Davis
Senior Production Designer: Larry Hunter
Publishing Systems Administrator: Rick Tucker
Production and Distribution Director: Phillip Lee
Associate Production Manager: Theresa L. Beste
Production Assistant: Faye Porter Bonner

Aleene's Creative Living
Founder: Aleene Jackson
Editor: Tiffany M. Windsor
Managing Editor: Cathy J. Burlingham
Assistant Editor: Joan Fee
Director of Photography: Craig Cook
Senior Photographer: Medeighnia Lentz
Designer/Stylist: Carolyn Bainbridge
Cover Portrait Photographer: Christine Photography

We're Here for You!
We at Oxmoor House are dedicated to serving you with reliable information that expands your imagination and enriches your life. We welcome your comments and suggestions. Please write us at:
Oxmoor House, Inc.
Editor, *Best of Aleene's Creative Living*
2100 Lakeshore Drive
Birmingham, AL 35209
To order additional publications, call 1-205-877-6560.

To order Aleene's products by mail, call Aleene's in California at 1-800-825-3363.

Projects pictured on cover (clockwise from top left): Pretty in Porcelain (page 26), Napkin Appliqué Casuals (page 84), Mosaic Masterpiece (page 42), and Tidings of Joy (page 106).

Contents

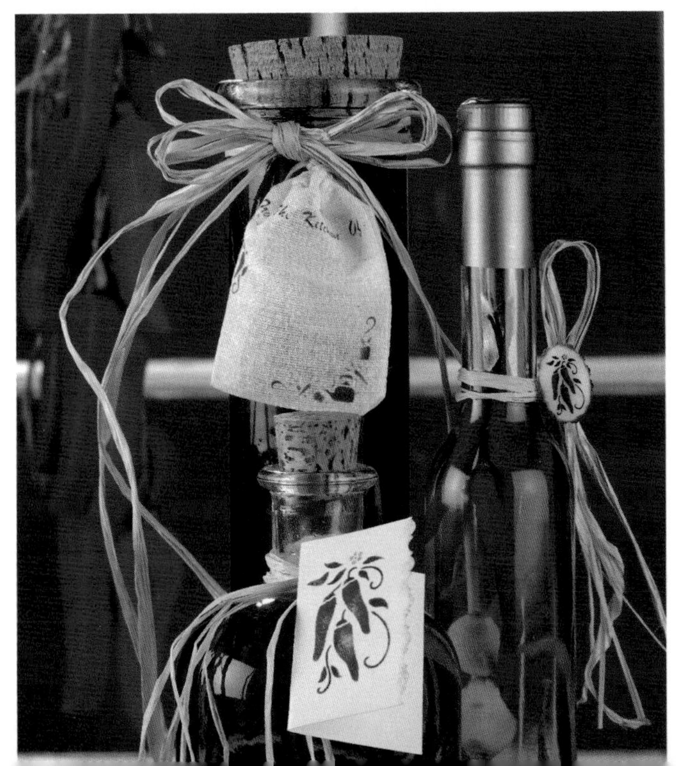

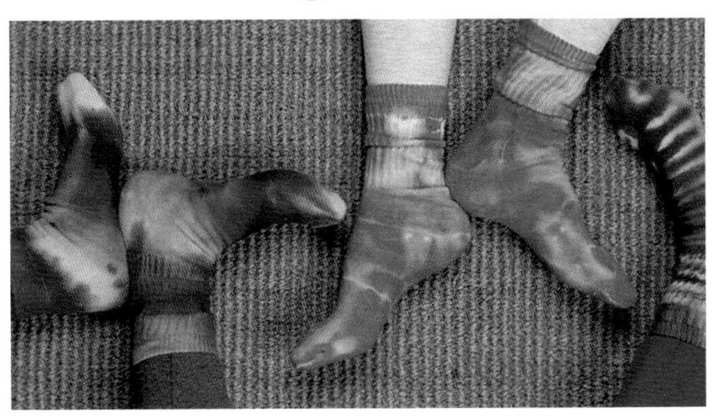

Introduction

We first introduced *Aleene's Creative Living* magazine as a weekly newsletter mini-magazine on October 3, 1992. It was conceived in a brainstorming session between my mother, Aleene, and my sister, Heidi. I undertook the task of writing and producing the magazine each week. In our first issue, we offered directions for two craft projects and a look behind the scenes at the "Creative Living" television show.

We quickly realized that we needed to expand the magazine to satisfy all the fans of the television show and provide them with directions for more crafts. Just a year after its launch, our mini-magazine had grown to a 68-page monthly that was a transcript of each month's television shows.

Today, we select about 40 ideas for each issue of the magazine from the more than 200 craft projects that are presented during a month of television shows. Because of the support and participation of national crafts stores and major manufacturers and the work of top independent designers, we are able to present our readers with fresh, new crafts featuring innovative products and brand-new techniques. From home decor, wearables, gifts, and holiday decorations, *Aleene's Creative Living* offers you the best in crafting ideas.

Now, we are delighted to have the opportunity to present you with the ***Best of Aleene's Creative Living,*** a carefully chosen selection of the outstanding ideas from past issues of the magazine. We hope you enjoy making these projects.

Wishing you endless creativity,

Tiffany

Crafting Hints

Tips for Successful Gluing

Aleene and Tiffany give you the benefit of their years of crafting experience with the following suggestions for working with glue.

• To make Aleene's Tacky Glue™ or Aleene's Designer Tacky Glue™ even tackier, leave the lid off for about an hour before use so that excess moisture evaporates.

• Too much glue makes items slip around; it does not provide a better bond. To apply a film of glue to a project, use a cardboard squeegee. Simply cut a 3" square of cardboard (cereal box cardboard works well) and use this squeegee to smooth the glue onto the craft material. Wait a few minutes to let the glue begin to form a skin before putting the items together.

• To squeeze fine lines of glue from a glue bottle, apply a temporary tape tip to the bottle nozzle. Using a 4"-long piece of transparent tape, align 1 long edge of the tape with the edge of the nozzle. Press the tape firmly to the nozzle to prevent leaks. Rotate the glue bottle to wrap the tape around the nozzle. The tape will reverse direction and wind back down toward the bottle. Press the tail of the tape to the bottle for easy removal.

Working with Aleene's Fusible Web

Wash and dry fabrics and garments to remove any sizing before applying fusible web. Do not use fabric softener in the washer or the dryer. Lay the fabric wrong side up on the ironing surface. A hard surface, like a wooden cutting board, will ensure a firmer bond. Lay the fusible web, paper side up, on the fabric (the glue side feels rough). With a hot, dry iron, fuse the web to the fabric by placing and lifting the iron. Do not allow the iron to rest on the web for more than 2 or 3 seconds. Do not slide the iron back and forth across the web.

Transfer the pattern to the paper side of the web and cut out the pattern as specified in the project directions. To fuse the cutout to the project, carefully peel the paper backing from the cutout, making sure the web is attached to the fabric. If the web is still attached to the paper, re-fuse it to the fabric cutout before fusing it to the project. Arrange the cutout on the project surface. With a hot, dry iron, fuse the cutout to the project by placing and lifting the iron. Hold the iron on each area of the cutout for approximately 60 seconds.

METRIC CONVERSION CHART

U.S.	Metric
⅛"	3 mm
¼"	6 mm
⅜"	9 mm
½"	1.3 cm
⅝"	1.6 cm
¾"	1.9 cm
⅞"	2.2 cm
1"	2.5 cm
2"	5.1 cm
3"	7.6 cm
4"	10.2 cm
5"	12.7 cm
6"	15.2 cm
7"	17.8 cm
8"	20.3 cm
9"	22.9 cm
10"	25.4 cm
11"	27.9 cm
12"	30.5 cm
36"	91.5 cm
45"	114.3 cm
60"	152.4 cm
⅛ yard	0.11 m
¼ yard	0.23 m
⅓ yard	0.3 m
⅜ yard	0.34 m
½ yard	0.46 m
⅝ yard	0.57 m
⅔ yard	0.61 m
¾ yard	0.69 m
⅞ yard	0.8 m
1 yard	0.91 m

To Convert to Metric Measurements:

When you know:	*Multiply by:*	*To find:*
inches (")	25	millimeters (mm)
inches (")	2.5	centimeters (cm)
inches (")	0.025	meters (m)
feet (')	30	centimeters (cm)
feet (')	0.3	meters (m)
yards	90	centimeters (cm)
yards	0.9	meters (m)

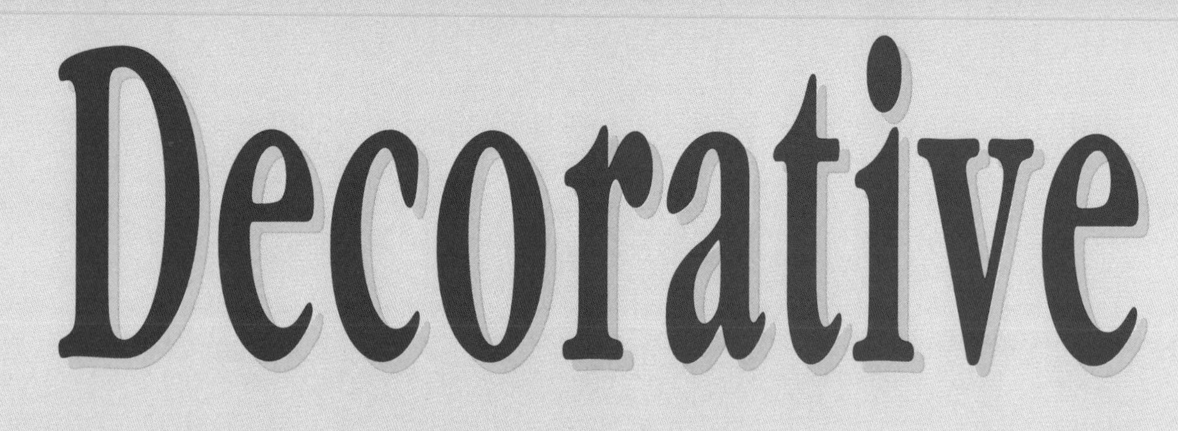

In the following pages, you'll find fantastic ideas for all sorts of fast and fun projects to decorate your home.

Page 24
Page 23
Page 20

Page 31

Accents

Materials

For each: 1 (12") length 16-gauge florist's wire
Needlenose pliers
26-gauge florist's wire

For 1 iris: 48" length 1½"-wide Offray Wire-Edge Ribbon: Purple Ombre
2 (12") lengths ⅞"-wide Offray Wire-Edge Ribbon: Green Ombre
Thread to match ribbons
3 (2") lengths yellow bump chenille stem
Aleene's Tacky Glue™
Green florist's tape

For 1 lily: 48" length 1½"-wide Offray Wire-Edge Ribbon: Pink Ombre
2 (12") lengths ⅞"-wide Offray Wire-Edge Ribbon: Green Ombre
Thread to match ribbons
Fine-tip permanent brown marker
Chenille stems: 6 (3") lengths yellow, 1 (3") length brown
Green florist's tape

For 1 tulip: 48" length 1½"-wide Offray Wire-Edge Ribbon: Deep Pink Ombre
2 (12") lengths ⅞"-wide Offray Wire-Edge Ribbon: Green Ombre
Thread to match ribbons
1 (3") length yellow chenille stem
Green florist's tape

For 1 forsythia branch: 2¼ yards ¼"-wide Offray Single-Face Satin Ribbon: Yellow
Brown florist's tape

Ribbons of Color

For this stunning bouquet, make irises, lilies, tulips, and forsythia branches from ribbons.

Directions

Note: To re-create arrangement shown in photo, make 3 irises, 3 lilies, 3 tulips, and 3 forsythia branches.

For each leaf or petal, cut specified length of ribbon. Fold ribbon in half widthwise (see Diagram A). Fold 2 top corners down at right angle (see Diagram B). Run gathering thread along top edge of ribbon from bottom point of 1 folded corner, across short straight edge, and down to bottom point of folded corner at other end (see Diagram B). Trim excess ribbon at each folded corner (see Diagram C). Pull thread to slightly gather ribbon. Secure thread. Open unstitched edge of ribbon and shape leaf or petal as desired (see photo).

For 1 iris, cut 6 (8") lengths of purple ribbon. Make 1 petal with each 8" ribbon length, stitching along dark edge of ribbon for 3 petals and stitching along light edge for remaining 3 petals. Make 1 leaf with each of 2 lengths of green ribbon.

Glue 1 bump chenille stem length along seam on right side of each dark petal (see photo). Let dry. With right sides facing, glue

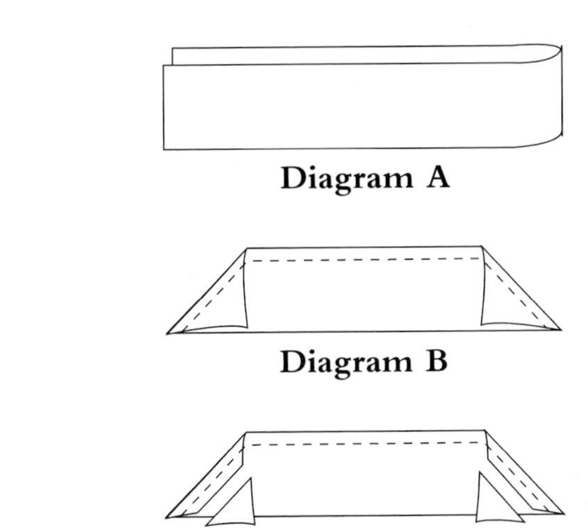

Diagram A

Diagram B

Diagram C

Designs by Offray

ends of 3 light petals together at tips to form top of iris. Let dry. Fold petals down with right sides out to form cupped part of iris.

Bend 1 end of 16-gauge wire for stem into small loop. Use 26-gauge wire to attach free end of cupped petals for top of iris to loop end of stem wire. With chenille side up, use 26-gauge wire to attach remaining petals to loop end of stem wire (see photo). Attach leaves to desired position on stem, using 26-gauge wire. Wrap bottom of iris and stem with green florist's tape, covering all wire.

For 1 lily, cut 6 (8") lengths from pink ribbon. Make 1 petal with each 8" ribbon length. Make 1 leaf with each of 2 lengths of green ribbon. Draw dots along center of each petal with marker (see photo). For center of lily, arrange 6 yellow chenille stem lengths around 1 brown chenille stem length. Handling all stem lengths as 1, wrap 1 end of bundle with 26-gauge wire to secure. Shape lily center as desired.

Bend 1 end of 16-gauge wire for stem into small loop. Use 26-gauge wire to attach lily center to loop end of stem wire. Use 26-gauge wire to attach 3 petals right side up to loop end of stem wire, spacing petals evenly around center. In same manner, attach remaining petals to stem. Attach leaves to desired position on stem, using 26-gauge wire. Wrap bottom of lily and stem with green florist's tape, covering all wire.

For 1 tulip, cut 6 (8") lengths of deep pink ribbon. Make 1 petal with each 8" ribbon length. Make 1 leaf with each of 2 lengths of green ribbon. Bend 1 end of 16-gauge wire for stem into small loop. Use 26-gauge wire to attach chenille stem length to loop end of stem wire. Coil free end of chenille stem to shape for tulip center. Use 26-gauge wire to attach 3 petals to loop end of stem wire, spacing petals evenly around center and arranging petals so that seam sides are toward center. In same manner, attach remaining petals to stem. Shape petals to form tulip. Attach leaves to desired position on stem, using 26-gauge wire. Wrap bottom of tulip and stem with green florist's tape, covering all wire.

For 1 forsythia branch, cut 40 (2") lengths of yellow ribbon. Cut 20 (4") lengths of 26-gauge wire. Handling 2 ribbon lengths as 1, fold ribbon lengths in half over 1 (4") length of wire. Twist wire to secure ribbon lengths. Repeat to make 20 blossoms. Use brown florist's tape to wrap bottom of each blossom and to attach blossoms to 16-gauge wire for branch, covering all wire.

Use wire-edged ribbon in variegated shades to create a bouquet of fancy flowers.

Flowery Frame

Quick-stitch these easy ribbon flowers and glue them onto a fabric-covered picture frame.

Design by Offray

Materials

Assorted widths Offray Wire-Edge Ribbon: Green and desired colors for flowers
Aleene's Designer Tacky Glue™ and low-temp hot-glue gun and glue sticks (See note.)
Thread to match ribbons for flowers
1 (2½"-diameter) bead or pom-pom for center of each flower
Fabric-covered picture frame

Directions

Note: To use Designer Tacky Glue in combination with glue gun, apply small amounts of each glue for strong and permanent bond.

For each stem, cut 1 (8") length of green ribbon. Tightly twist ribbon length between fingers to form stem of desired length. Apply 1 dot of glue to each end of stem to keep ribbon from untwisting.

For each leaf, cut 1 (5") length of green ribbon. Referring to Leaf Diagram, fold down ribbon ends to form leaf. Pinch and glue ribbon ends together. Let dry.

For flowers, cut 1 (10") length of desired color ribbon for each small flower and 1 (15") length of desired color ribbon for each large flower. Referring to Flower Diagram, measure and mark 2" sections on ribbon for small flower and 3" sections on ribbon for large flower. Run gathering thread along each ribbon as shown in Diagram. Pull thread to gather each ribbon into flower and secure thread. Glue bead or pom-pom to flower for center. Let dry.

Glue stems, leaves, and flowers to frame as desired. Let dry.

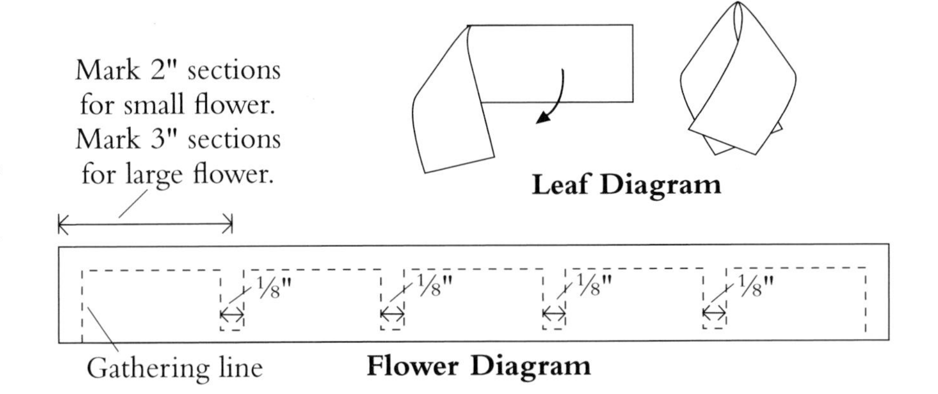

Leaf Diagram

Flower Diagram

MILLEFIORI MADE EASY

Purchased canes of clay make it easy to decorate frames and switchplates with mosaic-look designs. Here are the directions for the sunflower frame, but these same techniques apply to all the projects shown in the photo at left.

SUNFLOWER FRAME

Directions

1 Take frame apart and set small nails, backing, and glass aside. Following manufacturer's directions, condition confetti-patterned clay cane between hands until soft. Marbled lines of color will form. Roll cane with rolling pin or brayer to flatten. Cut 2 long narrow strips from flattened clay, using razor blade (see Photo A). Press each piece onto frame in desired position, using fingers to mold clay onto frame. Trim any excess clay with razor blade.

Materials

3" x 5" oval metal picture frame
Claymates Patterned Clay:
Sunflower pattern 3-pack
Rolling pin or brayer
Single-edge razor blade
Aleene's Gloss Right-On Finish™ or Aleene's Glaze-It™ (optional)
Sponge paintbrush (optional)

Photo A

Designs by Janet Kruk/Crooked River Crafts

2 Following manufacturer's directions, condition checked clay cane between hands until soft. Cut checked cane into thin slices. To slice, cut through cane with razor blade, rolling cane as you cut (see Photo B). Press each slice onto frame in desired position, using fingers to mold clay onto frame (see Photo C). In same manner, condition

Photo B

Photo C

sunflower cane and cut cane into thin slices. Press each sunflower slice onto frame in desired position, slightly overlapping previous clay pieces and pressing pieces together to completely cover frame (see Photo D). Smooth clay with fingers and fill in any remaining gaps with bits of leftover marbled clay. Poke holes in clay to match holes in frame, using small nails.

3 Place clay-covered frame on oven rack. Following manufacturer's directions, bake frame in 250° oven for 30 minutes. Let cool. If desired, brush 1 coat of finish on frame. Let dry. Assemble frame.

Photo D

Easy Elegance

Materials

Fine-grade sandpaper
Wooden tray
Aleene's Premium-Coat™ Acrylic Paints: Gold, Black
Paintbrushes: ½" flat shader, sponge
Aleene's Enhancers™: Mosaic Crackle Medium, Mosaic Crackle Activator
Floral gift wrap
Aleene's Instant Decoupage™ Glue

You can re-create this antique-look decoupaged tray in an afternoon.

Directions

1 Sand entire surface of tray. Mix equal parts Gold paint and Mosaic Crackle Medium. Paint tray with thick coat of Gold mixture. Let dry. Paint tray with thin to medium coat of Black paint. Let dry. Paint tray with thick coat of Mosaic Crackle Activator. Let dry.

2 Cut desired motifs from gift wrap. Working with 1 cutout at a time, apply coat of glue to wrong side of cutout. Press cutout onto tray in desired position. Brush coat of glue on top of cutout, pressing out any air bubbles. Repeat to glue additional cutouts to tray until you get desired effect. Let dry.

Design by Heidi Borchers, SCD/Aleene's

Cut the bottom edge of the cornice to scallop it. Glue tasseled trim along the edge to enhance the graceful curves.

Window Dressing

Cover lightweight foam-core board with fabric to make a fancy cornice for your window.

Materials

For each: **¼"-thick foam-core board (See Step 1.)**
Craft knife or large rotary cutter
Flexible quilter's curve (optional)
Aleene's Tacky Glue™
Craft fleece (See Step 2.)
Fabric (See Step 2.)
Assorted upholstery trims, ribbons, or contrasting fabric to decorate cornice (See Step 3.)
Aleene's Fusible Web™
2 angle brackets with screws
Screwdriver
Additional small screws

Directions for 1 cornice

Note: See page 5 for tips on working with fusible web.

1 To determine width of cornice, measure outside width of window, including any molding. Add 12" to that measurement. To determine length of cornice, measure length of window. Length of cornice should be about ⅙ of window length plus 4" for top of cornice. Cut foam-core board to these measurements, using craft knife or rotary cutter. (Be sure to cut foam-core board on protected work surface.) Referring to Diagram, cut away top corners and then score lines by cutting halfway through board. If desired, cut bottom edge of cornice to scallop, using flexible quilter's curve for guidance.

2 Cut 1 piece of fleece to cover 1 side of cornice, not including scored 1" at edge of each return. Glue fleece to right side (scored side) of cornice, leaving 1" at edge of each return uncovered (see Diagram). Let dry. Cut 1 piece of fabric to cover cornice, adding 2½" all around. Center cornice, fleece side down, on wrong side of fabric. Fold and glue excess fabric to wrong side of cornice, trimming corners and clipping curves as needed.

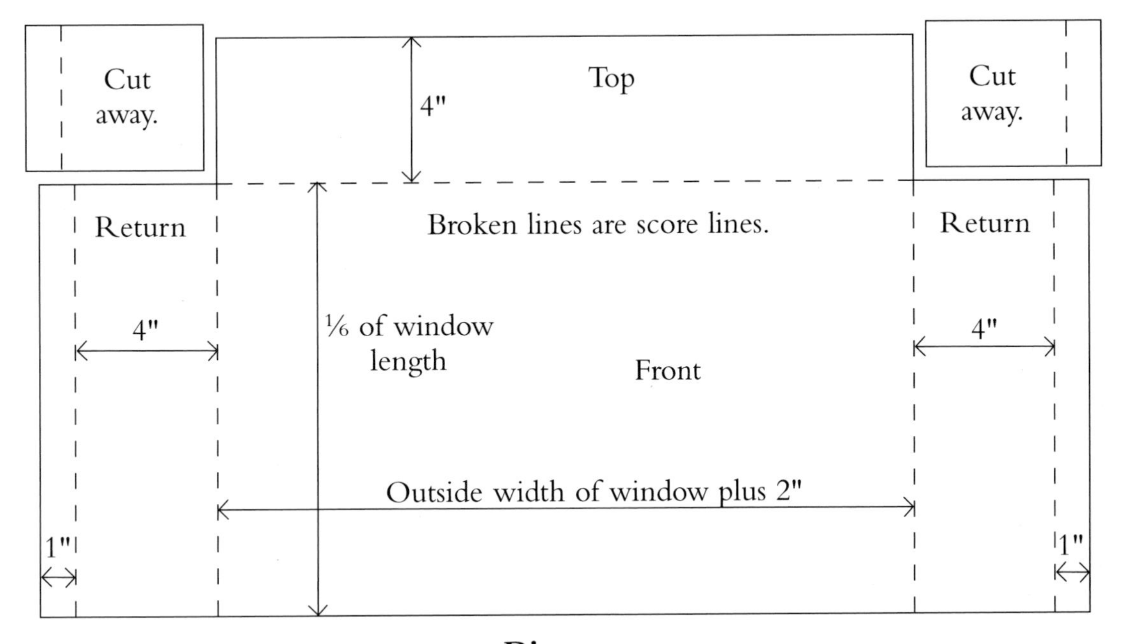

Diagram

Ribbon Cornice

3 To decorate cornice with upholstery trims (see photo on page 16), cut required length of trim and glue in place, pinning trim in place until glue is dry.

To decorate cornice with ribbons (see photo above), measure width of cornice, including returns, and add 4". Cut ribbon lengths to that measurement. Fuse web to wrong side of each ribbon length. Fuse ribbon lengths in place on cornice, fusing excess ribbon at each end to wrong side of cornice.

To decorate cornice with contrasting fabric (see photo below), measure width of cornice, including returns, and add 4". Measure height of front of cornice, not including top. Cut contrasting fabric to these measurements. Also cut 1 (4" x 5") piece for band from same contrasting fabric. Turn under ½" along each long edge of large fabric piece and glue or fuse for hem.

Referring to photo for positioning, center large fabric piece on front of cornice. Fold excess fabric at each end of cornice to wrong side and glue. Let dry. Turn under ½" along each 5" edge of 4" x 5" fabric piece and glue for hem. Gather center of contrasting fabric on cornice and wrap hemmed band around gathered area. Overlap ends of band at back of gathered fabric and pin to secure.

4 To assemble cornice, fold top, 1" returns, and 4" returns along scored lines to shape cornice. Pin returns and top together where they meet to secure. Attach angle brackets to wall above window. Rest cornice on brackets. Use additional screws to attach bottom of cornice to wall, inserting 1 screw through 1" return at each bottom edge of cornice.

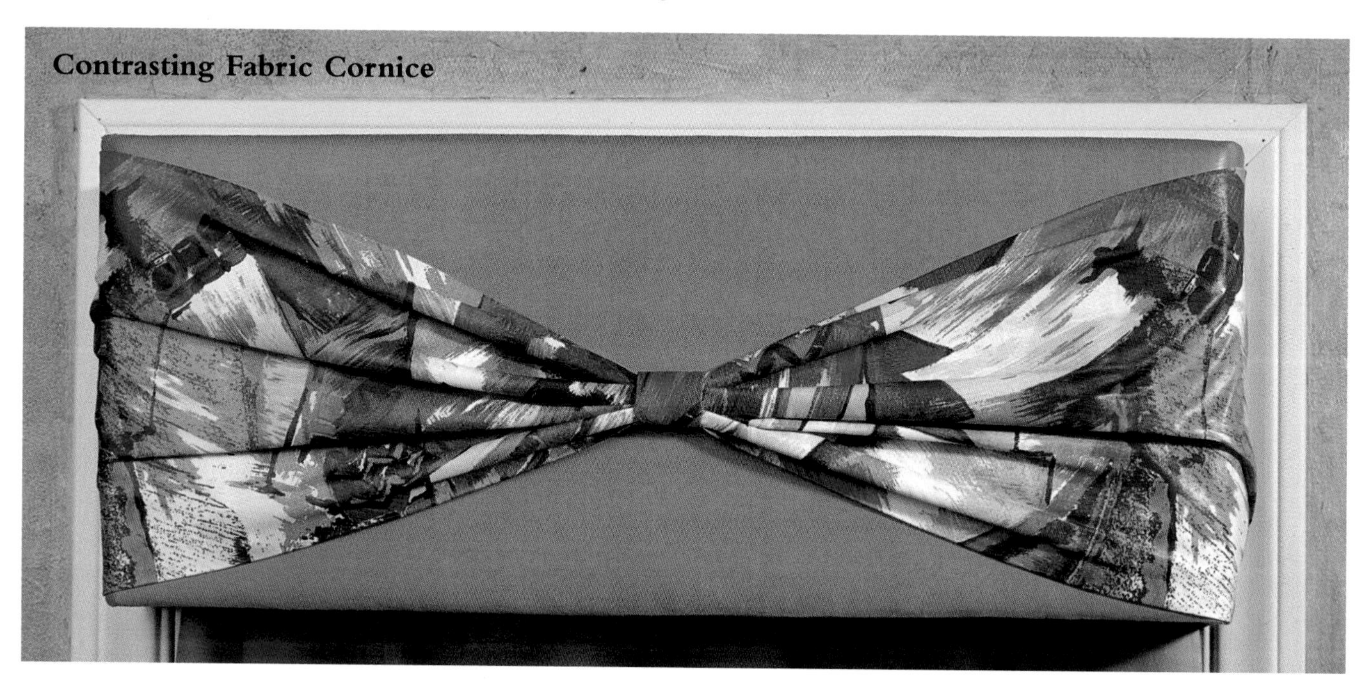

Contrasting Fabric Cornice

Designs by Darsee Lett and Pattie Donham/Hobby Lobby Stores

Decorate with Decoupage

Glue gift wrap onto canvas for a set of place mats and a matching rug.

Materials

For 1 place mat and 1 rug:
- **Cotton canvas: 1 (12" x 17") piece, 1 (21" x 28") piece**
- **Cardboard covered with waxed paper for work surface**
- **Sponge paintbrush**
- **Aleene's Instant Decoupage™ Glue**
- **Gift wrap: 1 (12" x 17") piece, 1 (21" x 28") piece**
- **¼"-diameter hole punch**
- **Natural raffia**
- **Large-eyed needle**

Directions

1 **For each,** tape canvas to cardboard covered with waxed paper. Brush generous coat of glue on 1 side of canvas. Press gift wrap into glue, gently pressing out any air bubbles. Paper may wrinkle; do not try to press out all wrinkles as paper will tear. Let dry. Brush coat of glue on top of paper. Let dry. Remove canvas from cardboard.

2 **For place mat,** trim 12" x 17" canvas to 11" x 16". Punch holes ½" from edge and ½" apart around edge of mat. Thread needle with several strands of raffia. Whipstitch raffia around edge of mat. Secure ends of raffia.

For rug, trim 21" x 28" canvas to 20" x 27". Punch holes ½" from edge and ½" apart along each 20" end of rug. Using several strands of raffia for each hole, make fringe across each end of rug.

All Wrapped Up

Dress up your chairs with cheerful fabric wraps. With this simple technique and seasonal or holiday fabrics, you can redecorate your dining room to suit all sorts of occasions.

Materials
For each: **2 yards 44"-wide woven fabric (See note.)**
Thread or Aleene's Fusible Web™
2 large safety pins
2 paper ribbon bows or other embellishments (See Step 4.)

Directions for 1 wrap

Note: Yardage given is for ladder-back chair shown in photo. Choose lightweight fabric that drapes well. Because wrong side of fabric will show, choose fabric with design woven into it.

See page 5 for tips on working with fusible web.

1 Measure over top of chair (see Diagram A). Add 2" to this measurement. Cut fabric to this length across full width of fabric. To hem raw edges, turn under ½" twice and stitch or fuse hems in place.

2 Drape fabric over chair. Catch selvage edges where fabric folds over chair back (see Diagram B). Bring selvages together at center back. Because covers fit loosely, 44" width of fabric may overlap at center by 1" or 2" or may leave slight gap where selvages will not quite meet. Either fit looks right.

3 Referring to Diagram B, pin selvages together at top edge and again just above seat, using large safety pins. Gather fabric at each front leg. Knot fabric behind spindle. Cover will drape loosely across seat.

4 Pin paper ribbon bows or other embellishments in place on cover to hide large safety pins. Other embellishments include bows made from wire-edged ribbon, pieces of costume jewelry, or small nosegays.

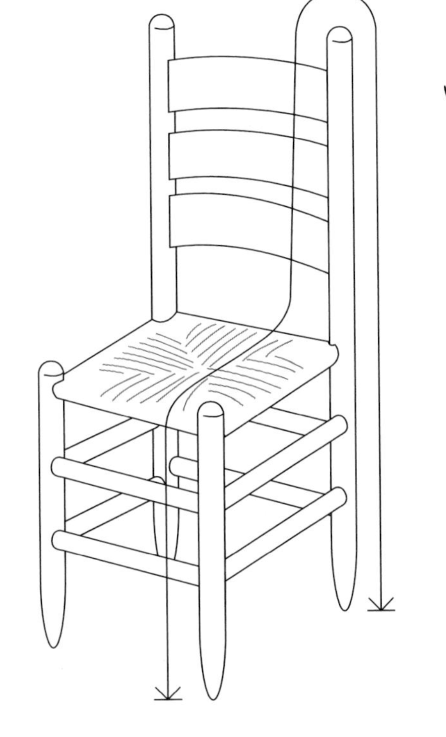

Diagram A

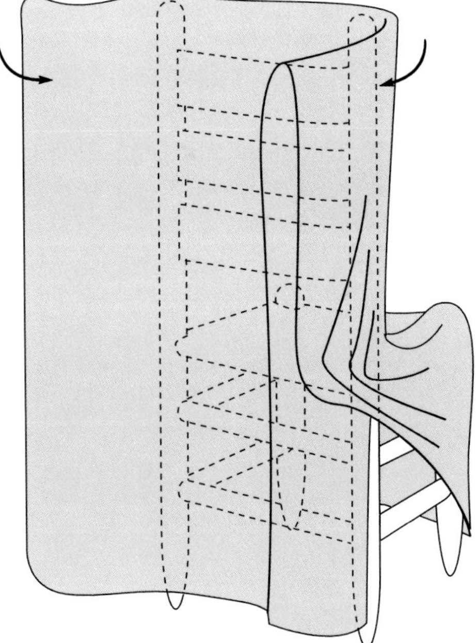

Diagram B

Design by Abigail Buckwald

Distinctive Decor

Stamp terrific designs onto all kinds of items to accent your home.

Materials

White lampshade
Washcloth
White place mat
Foam-core board for work surface
Picture frame
Deka Fabric paints: gold, silver, copper, black
Hot Potatoes Rubber Stamps: big swirl, fleur-de-lis, hoopla, small star, striped star
4 sponge paintbrushes
Cotton swabs

Directions

Note: To order Design Elements kit (containing gold, silver, copper, and black Deka Fabric paints; big swirl, fleur-de-lis, hoopla, small star, and striped star rubber stamps; and 2 sponge brushes), write or call Hot Potatoes, 209 10th Avenue South, Suite 311, Nashville, TN 37203; (615) 255-4055.

For lampshade, place 1 hand covered with washcloth inside shade and press washcloth against shade to stabilize area to be stamped.

For place mat, wash and dry mat; do not use fabric softener in washer or dryer. Lay mat on foam-core work surface.

To stamp designs on lampshade, place mat, or picture frame, dip 1 brush into desired color of paint. Apply even coat of paint to desired stamp. (*Note:* Use separate brush for each color of paint.) Wipe off excess paint around edges of stamp with cotton swab so that design will print clearly. Press stamp firmly onto item, being sure all areas of stamp come into contact with item. (*Hint:* Begin stamping near seam of lampshade and work in circles around shade for best effect.) Repeat to stamp additional designs onto item, applying fresh coat of paint after each stamping. Let dry.

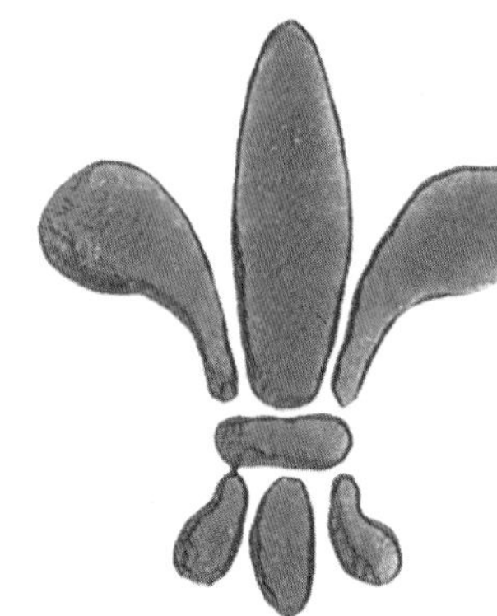
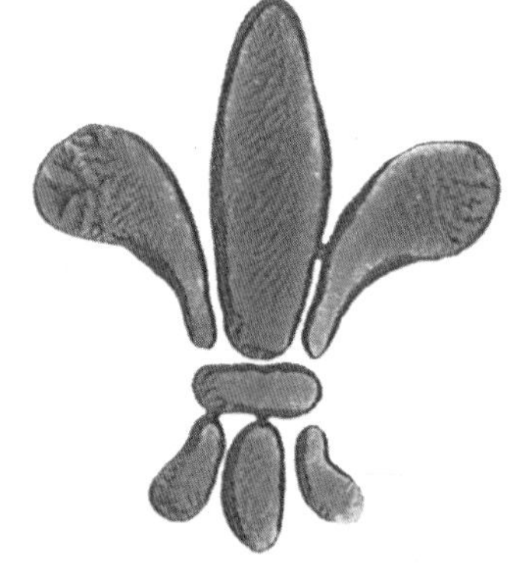
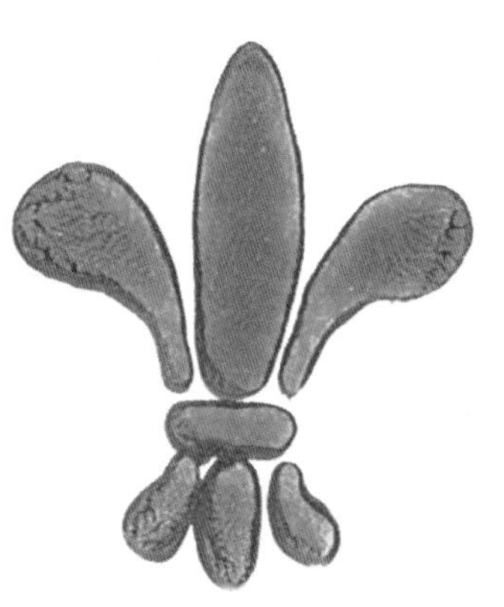

Designs by Mary O'Neil/Hot Potatoes

Angel to Love
Man to World
Boswell
Lavoisier
Fourier
Faraday
Hegel
Hegel
Ptolemy
Copernicus
Kepler
Plutarch
GREAT BOOKS
HORSES
and
TACK
ABC
DEF
GHI
JKL
MNO
PRS
TUV
WXY

Designs by Marlene Watson, SCD/House of Fabrics

Fruitful Stools

Glue fabric left over from your curtains to a wooden stool for a handy addition to the kitchen or bath.

Materials

For each: **Fine-grade sandpaper**
Wooden stool
Desired color Aleene's Premium-Coat™ Acrylic Paint
Flat shader paintbrush
¼ yard print fabric
Aleene's Fusible Web™
Aleene's Paper Napkin Appliqué™ Glue
1 yard ½"-wide flat braid to match fabric
Aleene's Designer Tacky Glue™
Aleene's Right-On™ Finish

Directions for 1 stool

Note: See page 5 for tips on working with fusible web.

1 Sand entire surface of stool. Paint stool with 1 or 2 coats of acrylic paint, letting dry between coats. To stabilize fabric, fuse web onto wrong side of fabric. Cut fabric to fit top of stool. Cut desired motifs from remaining fabric for legs of stool.

2 Brush Napkin Appliqué Glue on top of stool where fabric will be placed. Press fabric into glue, pressing out any air bubbles. Brush coat of Napkin Appliqué Glue on top of fabric. In same manner, glue cutouts to legs of stool as desired. Let dry. Apply 1 coat of Napkin Appliqué Glue to entire surface of stool. Let dry.

3 Glue braid to top of stool, covering raw edge of fabric, using Designer Tacky Glue. Let dry. Apply 2 coats of Right-On Finish to entire surface of stool, letting dry between coats.

Pretty in Porcelain

Stiffen silk flowers to make them durable and then paint them to look like fine porcelain.

Materials
Assorted silk flowers (See note.)
Basket with handle (See note.)
Aleene's Porcelain-Ize It™
Foam block covered with waxed paper (See Step 1.)
White spray paint
Aleene's Premium-Coat™ Acrylic Paints: assorted colors for flowers; Dusty Green, Deep Green, Ivory for leaves
Flat shader paintbrush
Waxed paper
Aleene's Designer Tacky Glue™
2 yards 2"-wide organdy ribbon

Directions

Note: Select flowers and basket in comparable sizes. For large basket, choose large flowers.

1 For each flower, dip flower into bowl filled with Porcelain-Ize It. Use fingers to squeeze excess Porcelain-Ize It from flower, removing as much as possible. Arrange petals so that they don't touch each other and shape flower as desired. Push stem of flower into waxed paper-covered foam. Let dry.

2 Spray-paint flower white. Let dry. Paint flower with desired base coat of acrylic paint. Let dry. For shading effect, double-load brush with paint by loading brush with base-coat paint, and then dipping 1 side of brush into first shade of paint. Stroke brush on waxed paper a few times to blend paints. With shade-color edge of brush at edge of petal, make 1 long, even stroke around edge of petal (see photo). Repeat to shade each petal of flower. (*Hint:* For shading on inner petals of flower, place shade-color edge of brush toward inside of flower to add depth.) Let dry.

3 For each leaf, dip leaf in Porcelain-Ize It, remove excess, and spray-paint white as described in steps 1 and 2. Paint leaf Dusty Green. Paint line of Deep Green around outer edge of leaf. Paint line of Ivory inside Deep Green line. Beginning at tip of leaf and working toward center vein, draw brush through both lines of paint to blend colors. After each stroke, wipe brush on paper towel to remove excess paint. To complete leaf, lightly paint thin line of Deep Green down center of leaf for vein. Let dry.

4 Glue flowers in place on basket handle. Cut 2 (1-yard) lengths from ribbon. Tie each ribbon length in bow. Glue 1 bow at each end of basket handle. Trim streamers to desired length and notch ends. Let dry.

Double-load your paintbrush with paint to get a delicate shaded effect on the flower.

Design by Heidi Borchers, SCD/Aleene's

Please
Call Beth
Tuesday
Appointments
Addresses
N O E L

QUILTING for efficiency

Organize your home office with this punch-quilted wall hanging. Handy pockets and wooden spools keep all your tools exactly where you need them.

Materials

Hunt X-ACTO® Small Rotary Cutter and Self Healing Cutting Mat
Assorted print fabrics: 1 (16" x 33") piece, 1 (13" x 15") piece, 1 (13" x 28") piece
1 (15") square ½"-thick Hunt Beinfang® foam board
Hunt X-ACTO® Craft Board Cutter
1 (15" x 20") piece batting
Aleene's Designer Tacky Glue™ and hot-glue gun and glue sticks (See note.)
Hunt X-ACTO® Burnisher/Fabric Punch
2 (3") lengths ⅛"-wide Wrights® satin ribbon to match fabrics
1 (14½") square white posterboard
62" length ½"-wide braided trim
3 (¾") cup hooks
4 (⅝" x ¾") Wang's wooden spools
4 (30") lengths embroidery floss to match fabrics
4 (1") lengths 3mm-diameter Forster wooden dowel

Directions

Note: To use Designer Tacky Glue in combination with glue gun, apply small amounts of each glue for strong and permanent bond.

1 Use rotary cutter and cutting mat to cut all fabrics. From 16" x 33" piece of fabric, cut 1 (6") square and 1 (7") square for 1 pocket; 1 (16") square for back; 10 (2½") squares, each cut in half diagonally for a total of 20 triangles, for quilted design; and 5 (2½" x 3½") rectangles for edges of quilted design. From 13" x 15" piece of fabric, cut 1 (6") square and 1 (7") square for 1 pocket; 11 (2½") squares, each cut in half diagonally for a total of 22 triangles, for quilted design; and 2 (2½" x 3½") rectangles for edges of quilted design. From 13" x 28" piece of fabric, cut 1 (6") square and 1 (7") square for 1 pocket; 2 (3½") squares for top corners of quilted design; 18 (2½") squares for quilted design; and 10 (2½" x 3½") rectangles for edges of quilted design.

2 Referring to Organizer Diagram, mark score lines on 1 side of foam board. Cut ¼"-deep score lines along all marked lines, using board cutter. Cut 2 pieces of batting to fit each area

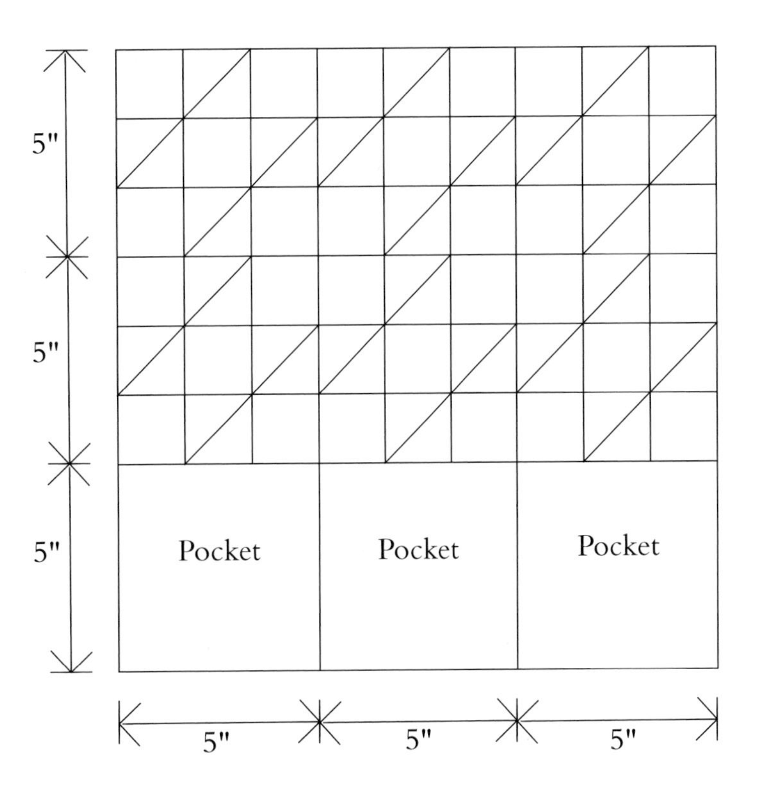

Organizer Diagram

Design by Cindy Groom Harry® and Staff/Hunt Manufacturing Co.

of design except pockets. With edges aligned with score lines, stack and glue 2 pieces of batting in place on foam board. Let dry.

3 To punch fabric pieces into board, center 1 fabric piece over matching batting shape. Press excess fabric into board along score lines, using flat side of burnisher. Begin with interior design areas. Trim corners of fabric as needed. For each exterior triangle, use 1 (2½" x 3½") rectangle of fabric, trimming fabric to fit as needed. Fold and tape or glue excess fabric to back of board. Use 1 (7") square of fabric to cover each pocket area. Use 3½" squares at top corners of quilted design area.

4 For hanger loops, fold each ribbon length in half to form loop. Glue ends to back of organizer at top, 5" from each corner. Let dry. Center and glue 16" square of fabric to cover 1 side of posterboard. Fold and glue excess fabric to back of posterboard. Center and glue fabric-covered posterboard to back of organizer, being sure hangers extend beyond edge. Let dry.

5 Turn under ½" along 2 opposite edges of each 6" square of fabric for top and bottom of pocket. Referring to Pocket Diagram, turn under side edges of each piece, turning under ¼" at top corners of pocket and increasing to ½" at bottom corners, and glue. Let dry. Glue each pocket in place on front of organizer, positioning top corners to allow room for items to be put into pocket. Let dry. Glue braided trim around edge of organizer. Carefully screw 1 cup hook into bottom edge of organizer, centering screw below 1 pocket. Remove hook. Dip screw of hook into glue and reinsert into edge of organizer. Repeat to attach 1 hook below each pocket.

6 Wrap and glue 1 floss length to cover each spool. Let dry. To attach each spool to organizer, push 1 dowel into organizer in desired position (see photo). Be sure to insert dowel between areas of quilted design. Remove dowel. Dip end of dowel into glue and reinsert into organizer. Apply glue to free end of dowel. Push spool onto dowel. Let dry.

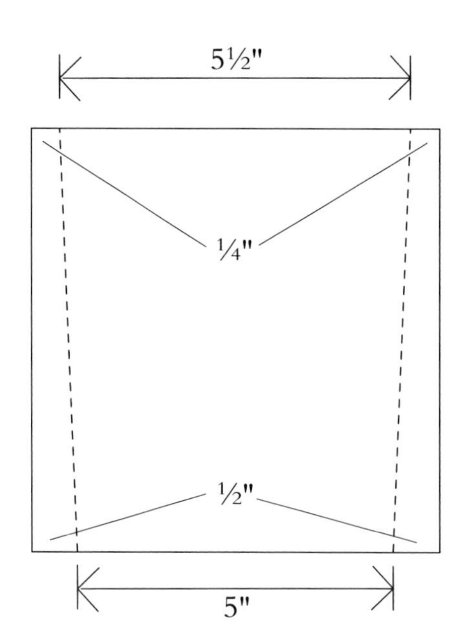

Pocket Diagram

Garden Wreath

Touches of gold highlight the trowel and flowerpot used in this wreath. Seed packets, artificial vegetables, and a bow made from a pair of garden gloves complete the design.

Design by Tracia Ledford, SCD, CPD/Delta Technical Coatings

Materials

Delta Renaissance Foil: Antique Gold Kit (base coat, adhesive, foil, antique, and sealer)
Hand trowel
Paintbrush
2½"-diameter clay pot
1 pair garden gloves
18-gauge florist's wire
15"-long oval grapevine wreath
Green Spanish moss
Aleene's Designer Tacky Glue™
5 seed packets
Assorted dried flowers (wreath shown uses tapestry millet, linen gypsophila, and pink pepper berries)
Assorted miniature plastic vegetables
2" mushroom bird
2 artificial bumblebees
1 artificial butterfly

Directions

1 Paint shovel of trowel with Renaissance base coat. Let dry. Paint shovel of trowel and outside of pot with uneven coat of Renaissance adhesive. Let dry until clear. To apply gold foil, lay foil dull side down on top of adhesive-covered area. Using finger, press foil onto adhesive. Peel away foil paper. If any part of adhesive is not covered, reapply foil as needed. Brush Renaissance antique on shovel of trowel. Wipe off excess with paper towel. Let dry. Apply 1 coat of Renaissance sealer to shovel of trowel and outside of pot. Let dry.

2 With palm side down, fold cuff of 1 glove over toward back of glove and glue to make loop for center of bow. Slip wire through loop of glove. With palm sides down and fingers pointing in opposite direction, attach remaining glove behind glove with loop to form bow, twisting wire ends tightly to gather center of bow and arranging fingers as desired (see photo). Attach glove bow to top of wreath, using wire tails.

3 Working with wreath as if it were a clock, glue Spanish moss to cover area of wreath from 4:00 position to 9:00, using Designer Tacky Glue. Let dry. Attach trowel and clay pot to wreath, using wire and Designer Tacky Glue. Referring to photo for positioning, glue seed packets and all remaining items to wreath. Let dry.

Chicken Chimes

Paint flowerpots and glue on trims to make this cute pair of windchimes to brighten your porch.

Materials

For each: **Aleene's Instant Decoupage™ Glue (matte)**
Sponge paintbrush
Aleene's Premium-Coat™ Acrylic Paint: True Yellow
Aleene's Designer Tacky Glue™
Orange Fun Foam scrap
Fine-tip permanent black marker
Yellow craft feathers
¼"-diameter hole punch
2 (1½"-diameter) jingle bells

For large chick: **6"-diameter clay pot**
72" length yellow twisted paper
Straw hat to fit bottom of pot
8" length ¼"-wide green picot-edge ribbon
18" length 1"-wide orange grosgrain ribbon

For small chick: **3"-diameter clay pot**
36" length twine
4" length ¼"-wide green picot-edge ribbon
8" length 1"-wide orange grosgrain ribbon
Yellow twisted paper scrap

Directions

1 **For each,** apply 1 coat of Decoupage Glue to entire surface of pot. Let dry. Paint entire surface of pot True Yellow. Let dry.

For large chick, fold twisted paper in half. Tie overhand knot in paper twist about 10" from folded end. Working from inside pot, thread folded end of paper through hole in bottom of pot. Center and cut small hole in top of hat. Thread folded end of paper through hole in hat and slide hat down on top of pot. Knot folded paper just above hat. Glue first knot inside pot. Glue hat to pot. Let dry. Referring to photo, fold up hat brim and glue, pinning brim in place until glue is dry.

For small chick, fold twine in half. Tie overhand knot in twine about 6" from folded end. Working from inside pot, thread folded end of twine through hole in bottom of pot. Knot twine just above pot. Glue first knot inside pot. Let dry.

2 **For each,** transfer pattern to Fun Foam and cut 1 beak and 2 feet. Referring to photo, draw details on large beak, small beak, and small feet, using marker. Draw eyes on pot, using marker. Referring to photo, glue beak in place on chick. Glue feathers and green ribbon on chick. Tie orange ribbon in bow and glue bow in place on chick. Let dry.

3 Punch 1 hole in each foot (see photo). Thread 1 foot and 1 jingle bell on each free end of hanger below chick, knotting hanger to secure bell and foot.

For small chick, untwist yellow twisted paper scrap and cut 2 (3") pieces. Glue 1 paper piece on each side of small chick for wings.

Small Beak

Small Foot

Large Foot

Large Beak

Designs by Northwest Fabrics and Crafts

Dapper Decoys

Pinecone and wheat pieces and pumpkin seeds become feathers on these decoy ducks.

Materials

For each: **Decoy duck with glass eyes**
Aleene's Designer Tacky Glue™
Assorted colors Aleene's Premium-Coat™ Acrylic Paint
Paintbrush
Assorted sizes pinecones
Wire cutters or tin snips
Toothpicks
Pumpkin seeds
Wheat
Aleene's Gloss Right-On Finish™
Sponge paintbrush
Brown felt

Directions for 1 duck

1 Glue eyes in place on duck. Paint bill with desired colors of acrylic paint. Let dry. Using wire cutters or tin snips, cut scales from pinecones.

2 Beginning at tail and working over 1 section of duck at a time, brush even coat of glue on duck. Let dry 10 minutes. Use toothpick to apply glue to each item to be placed on duck. Refer to photo for placement of items. Glue pinecone scales, pumpkin seeds, and wheat to cover duck, overlapping rows slightly. For best effect, completely cover duck with items (see photo). Let dry.

3 Brush duck with 1 or 2 coats of Right-On Finish, letting dry between coats. Be sure to apply finish between layers to completely seal items. Cut felt to fit bottom of duck. Glue felt to bottom of duck. Let dry.

Design by Marlene Watson, SCD/Aleene's

Wood Twist Wreath

Curly wood shavings in various shades of brown give this wreath lots of texture.

Materials

Keenan straw wreath
Paper ribbon
Aleene's Designer Tacky Glue™ and hot-glue gun and glue sticks (See note.)
1½ yards each 1½"-wide pink satin ribbon, 2"-wide pink organdy ribbon
⅓ yard 4"-wide gold mesh ribbon
22-gauge florist's wire
Assorted silk flowers and ferns
Euna's Wood Twists
Hairpins or T-pins

Directions

Note: To use Designer Tacky Glue in combination with glue gun, apply small amounts of each glue for strong and permanent bond.

Wrap wreath with paper ribbon to prevent straw from shedding. Glue ends of ribbon to secure. Make 1 multilooped bow with each pink ribbon length, securing each bow with florist's wire. Glue bows, silk flowers, and silk ferns in place on wreath (see photo). Let dry. Cover remainder of wreath with wood twists, using hair pins or T-pins to attach twists to wreath.

Design by Jo-Ann Fabrics and Crafts

Design by Heidi Borchers, SCD/Aleene's

Garden Decoupage

Give your favorite houseplant a new home by gluing gift-wrap cutouts to a clay flowerpot.

Materials

Clay pot and saucer
Gold spray paint
Garden motif or floral gift wrap
Sponge paintbrush
Aleene's Instant Decoupage™ Glue (matte)
Aleene's Designer Tacky Glue™
Green moss
Plastic wrap
Natural raffia
12" length 1"-wide organdy ribbon
Assorted dried flowers and foliage

Directions

Note: For best results, use plastic liner inside decoupaged pot.

1 Spray-paint pot and saucer gold. Let dry. Cut desired motifs from gift wrap. Working with 1 gift-wrap cutout at a time, brush Decoupage Glue on wrong side of cutout. Press cutout onto pot in desired position. Brush coat of Decoupage Glue on top of cutout, pressing out any air bubbles. Repeat to glue additional cutouts to pot until you get desired effect, leaving rim uncovered. Let dry. Brush coat of Decoupage Glue over entire surface of pot. Let dry.

2 Apply even coat of Designer Tacky Glue around rim of pot. Press moss into glue around rim of pot. Cover moss with plastic wrap, stretching plastic wrap tightly over moss, to hold moss in place until glue is dry. Remove plastic wrap.

3 Measure around rim of pot on top of moss. Add 10" to that measurement. Cut several lengths of raffia to that measurement. Handling all raffia lengths as 1, knot raffia lengths around rim of pot on top of moss. Trim raffia streamers as desired. Tie ribbon in bow. Glue bow and assorted dried flowers and foliage to rim of pot on top of raffia knot. Let dry.

Pick a Pocket

Materials

3 (½-yard) pieces assorted Homespun Fabrics
3 (5" x 6¼") pieces Warm and Natural Batting
Pearl cotton thread to match fabrics
Aleene's Tacky Glue™
Raffia
Assorted buttons
2 small stuffed fabric sunflowers
Poly-fil® stuffing
2 small stuffed fabric crows
1 package dried orange slices
5 mini-stem silk sunflowers
1 small painted wooden sunflower

Directions

1 Cut 9 (5" x 6¼") pieces from assorted fabrics. For 1 pocket, stack 1 fabric piece right side down, 1 batting piece, and 2 more fabric pieces right side up. Fold down 1" along top short edge of top fabric piece. With pearl cotton thread, baste around all raw edges of pocket, using ¼" seam allowance and stitching through all layers. Fringe fabric edges. Repeat to make another pocket. In same manner, stack remaining fabric pieces for third pocket. Referring to photo, trim edges of 1 pocket and flap for center of garland. Blanket-stitch around raw edges of pocket and flap, using pearl cotton thread.

2 For each pocket, tear 1 (1¼" x 12") strip of fabric. Knot ends of fabric strip. Glue knots to top corners of pocket for handle. Let dry.

3 Transfer pattern to fabric and cut 1 small heart. Fringe edges of heart. Cut 1 (10") length of raffia. Tie raffia in bow. Glue fabric heart, raffia bow, and assorted buttons to 1 pocket with fringed edges (see pocket at left

Tuck stuffed shapes, silk and wood flowers, seed packets, and dried oranges into the pockets of this garland.

Design by Rebecca Hermann/Jo-Ann Fabrics and Crafts

Large Heart

Small Heart

in photo). Cut 4 (1¼" x 3") strips of fabric. Stack strips to form fabric flower (see pocket at right in photo). Cut 1 (14") length of pearl cotton thread. Tie thread in bow around strips, threading 1 button on thread ends (see photo). Cut 1 (10") length of raffia. Tie raffia in bow. Glue fabric flower and raffia bow to remaining pocket with fringed edges. Glue 1 stuffed fabric sunflower and assorted buttons to blanket-stitched pocket. Let dry. Place small amount of stuffing in each pocket.

4 Transfer pattern to fabric and cut 4 large hearts. With wrong sides facing and raw edges aligned, baste 2 hearts together, using pearl cotton thread and stuffing heart lightly before stitching is complete. Repeat to make second heart.

5 Tear 1 (1¼" x 36") strip of fabric. Cut 1 (36") length each of pearl cotton thread and raffia. For garland, braid fabric strip, pearl cotton thread length, and raffia, knotting ends to secure braid. Tear 2 (1½" x 22") strips of fabric. Tie 1 strip in bow around braid at each end of garland. Cut 9 (10") lengths of raffia. Tie each length in bow to attach pocket handles and 6 orange slices to garland (see photo). Glue large hearts to garland between pockets. Cut 2 (8") lengths of pearl cotton thread. Tie each length in bow. Glue 1 bow and 1 small silk sunflower to each heart. Let dry.

6 Tuck and glue remaining items inside pockets of garland. Let dry.

Handmade

Show off your creative talents with this selection of quick and easy gifts to craft.

Presents

Mosaic MASTERPIECE

Colorful paper squares and gold foiling give a glass hurricane the look of stained glass.

Materials

Assorted colors 1-ply gossamer paper napkins or tissue paper
Glass hurricane
Masking tape
1"-wide soft-bristle paintbrush
Aleene's Reverse Collage™ Glue
Aleene's 3-D Foiling™ Glue
Aleene's Gold Crafting Foil™

Directions

1 Cut paper napkins or tissue paper into 1" squares. Wrap 1 piece of tape around center on outside of hurricane for placement guide. Working over small area at a time, brush coat of Reverse Collage Glue on inside of hurricane. Using tape as guide and arranging colors as desired, press paper squares into glue, forming horizontal rows. Brush coat of Reverse Collage Glue on top of paper, pressing out any air bubbles. Remove tape.

2 Working on outside of hurricane, outline each paper square with lines of 3-D Foiling Glue. Let dry. (Glue will be opaque and sticky when dry. Glue must be thoroughly dry before foil is applied.) To apply gold foil, lay foil dull side down on top of glue lines. Using finger, gently but firmly press foil onto glue, completely covering glue with foil. Peel away foil paper. If any part of glue is not covered, reapply foil as needed.

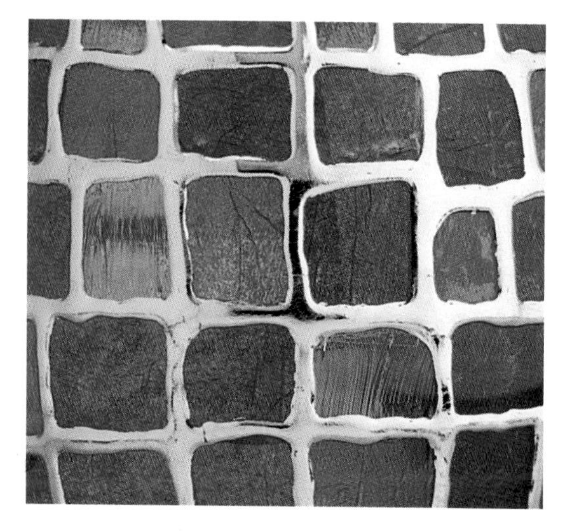

Design by Darsee Lett and Pattie Donham/Hobby Lobby Stores

Flowerpot TEA TOWELS

Fuse fabric cutouts onto purchased towels to make these kitchen accents.

Materials
***For each:* 1 green plaid towel**
Assorted print fabric scraps
Aleene's Ultra-Hold Fusible Web™

Directions for 1 towel

Note: See page 5 for tips on working with fusible web.

Wash and dry towel and fabrics; do not use fabric softener in washer or dryer. Fuse web onto wrong side of fabric scraps. Transfer patterns to scraps and cut 1 pot, 4 flowers, 4 centers, and 8 leaves. Referring to photo for positioning, arrange cutouts on towel and fuse in place. Do not wash towel for at least 1 week. Wash by hand and hang to dry.

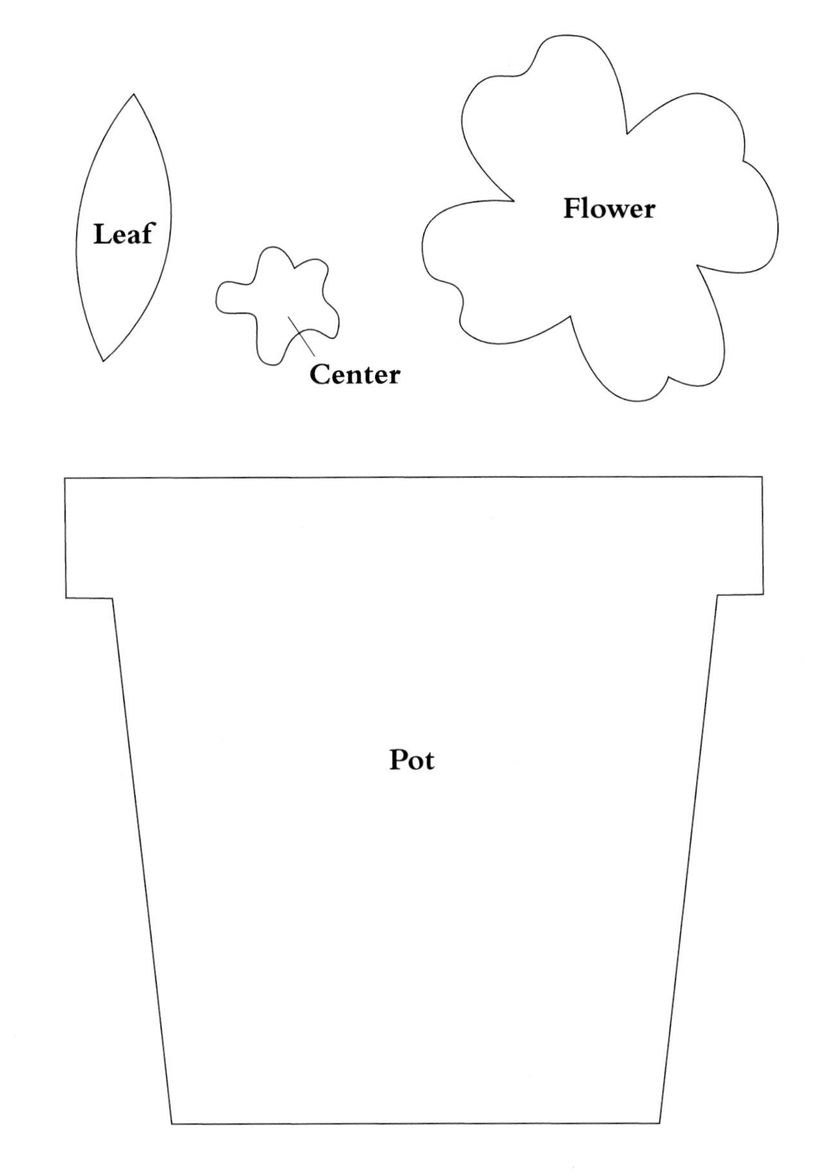

Designs by Trena Hegdahl/Aleene's

Floral Express

Materials
For each: **2 (2" x 3" x 1½") blocks florist's foam**
Mailbox Huggie frame by H & D Designs
Florist's tape
Florist's picks
Silk or dried greenery and flowers
Aleene's Designer Tacky Glue™
Artificial pinecones
Seasonal decorative picks
Spanish moss
4 yards weatherproof ribbon (optional)
Florist's wire

Design by Jo-Ann Fabrics and Crafts

Add a silk or dried floral swag to your mailbox. Create a different swag to suit each season.

Directions for 1 swag

Press blocks of florist's foam onto prongs of Huggie frame, placing foam ½" above the tie-down hole on side of frame. Tape foam to frame for added stability. Attach silk greenery to florist's picks as needed, using florist's tape. Dip each item into glue and push into foam to create arrangement. See photo for ideas. Glue Spanish moss to cover exposed areas of foam. Let dry. If desired, tie ribbon in bow and secure bow with florist's wire. Attach bow to arrangement. Attach 1 piece of wire to each tie-down hole on frame, leaving long tails. Place frame on mailbox and tightly twist wire tails together below box.

Design by Heather McDonald/The Beadery

Heart's Desire

Trim a heart-shaped trinket box with lace, braid, and a puffy fabric heart for this lovely Mother's Day gift.

Materials

Heart Adornables™ box by The Beadery
2 (6") squares textured fabric
Aleene's Designer Tacky Glue™ and hot-glue gun and glue sticks (See note.)
12" length ⅝"-wide pregathered lace trim
12" length ⅛"-wide satin ribbon
12" length ½"-wide braid
1" square batting
Heart charm with center cutout
4" square satin

Directions

Note: To use Designer Tacky Glue in combination with glue gun, apply small amounts of each glue for strong and permanent bond.

1 Center and glue box on wrong side of 1 (6") fabric square by placing dots of glue around edge of box and pressing fabric into glue. Be sure fabric lies flat against box. Trim fabric even with rim. Repeat to glue remaining 6" fabric square to lid.

2 Beginning at top center of heart and with bound edge of lace aligned with rim of box, glue lace around box. Let dry. Beginning at top center of heart, glue ribbon around box to cover bound edge of lace. Let dry. Beginning at top center of heart and with 1 edge of braid aligned with rim of lid, glue braid around lid. Let dry.

3 Center and glue batting square on fabric-covered lid. Using charm as guide, trim satin slightly smaller than charm. Apply glue around edge on wrong side of trimmed satin piece. Center satin over batting and glue in place on lid. Let dry. Center and glue charm over satin so that batting puffs up inside cutout. Let dry.

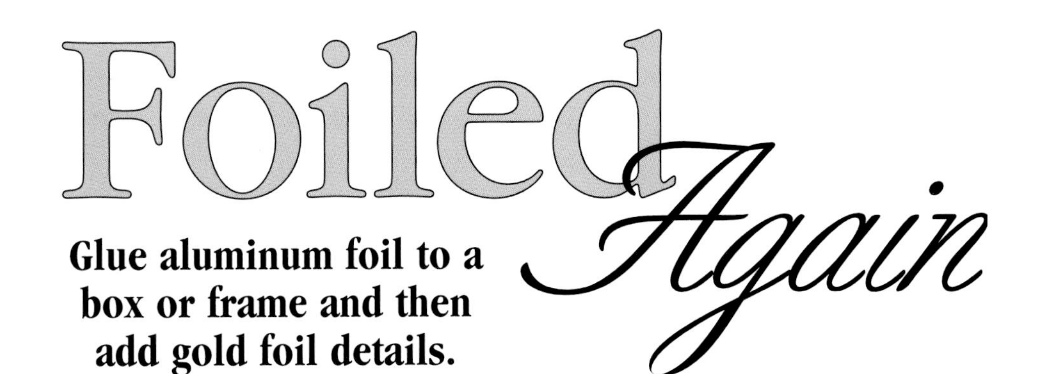

Foiled Again

Glue aluminum foil to a box or frame and then add gold foil details.

Materials
Frame
Round box
Aluminum foil
2" square cardboard squeegee
Aleene's Tacky Glue™
Rolling pin or brayer
Aleene's 3-D Foiling™ Glue
Aleene's Gold Crafting Foil™

Directions

1 **For frame,** cut 1 piece of aluminum foil a bit larger than frame, being careful not to wrinkle foil. Cut opening in foil, leaving at least ½" around inside of frame. Squeegee coat of glue on right side of frame. Place foil over glued area. Press foil with rolling pin to smooth. Fold excess foil around inner and outer edges to back of frame and glue. Let dry.

For box, in same manner, glue aluminum foil to cover box and lid.

2 **For each,** apply lines and dots of 3-D Foiling Glue to piece as desired. Let dry. (Glue will be opaque and sticky when dry. Glue must be thoroughly dry before foil is applied.) To apply gold foil, lay foil dull side down on top of glue design. Using finger, gently but firmly press foil onto glue, completely covering glue with foil. Peel away foil paper. If any part of glue is not covered, reapply foil as needed.

Designs by Heidi Borchers, SCD/Aleene's

Country at Heart

Buttons and fabric yo-yos give this stuffed heart lots of rustic charm.

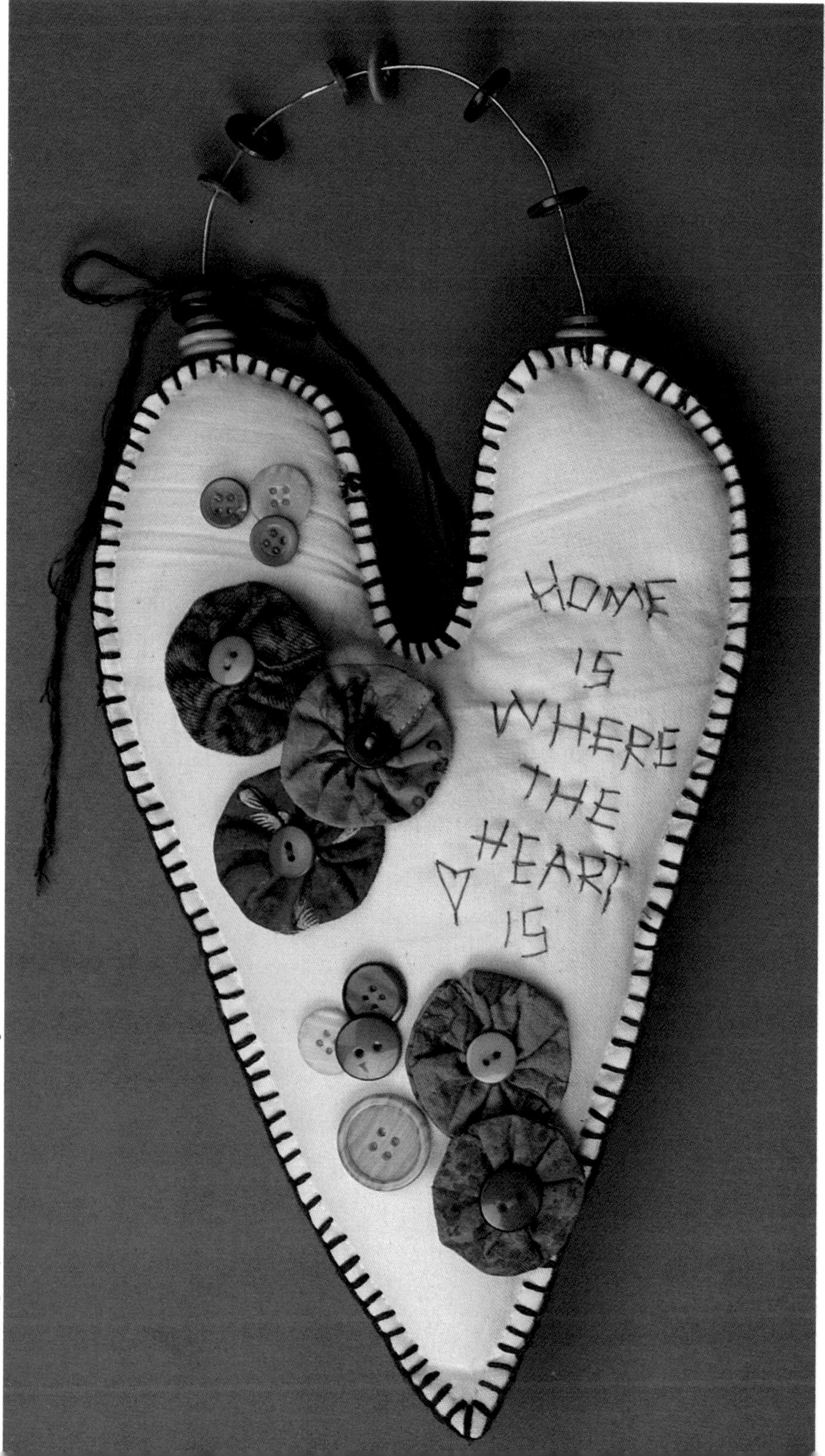

Design by Jo-Ann Fabrics and Crafts

Materials
2 (9" x 12") pieces muslin
Thread to match
Stuffing
Large-eyed needle
Dark green pearl cotton thread
14" length 18-gauge florist's wire
Assorted buttons
Gold embroidery floss
Westwater yo-yos: 5 in assorted colors
Aleene's Designer Tacky Glue™

Directions

1 Transfer pattern to muslin and cut 2 hearts. Using ¼" seam allowance, stitch hearts together, leaving small opening for turning. Clip curves and turn. Stuff heart. Slipstitch opening closed. Blanket-stitch around edge of heart, using large-eyed needle and dark green pearl cotton thread.

2 Shape florist's wire for handle to fit heart (see photo). Thread several buttons on wire. Poke wire ends into heart at top. Bend up wire ends at back of heart to secure. Referring to photo, embroider small heart and "Home is where the heart is" with gold floss. Glue or stitch yo-yos and buttons on heart. Let glue dry. Cut 1 (14") length of green pearl cotton. Tie green pearl cotton in bow around wire handle (see photo).

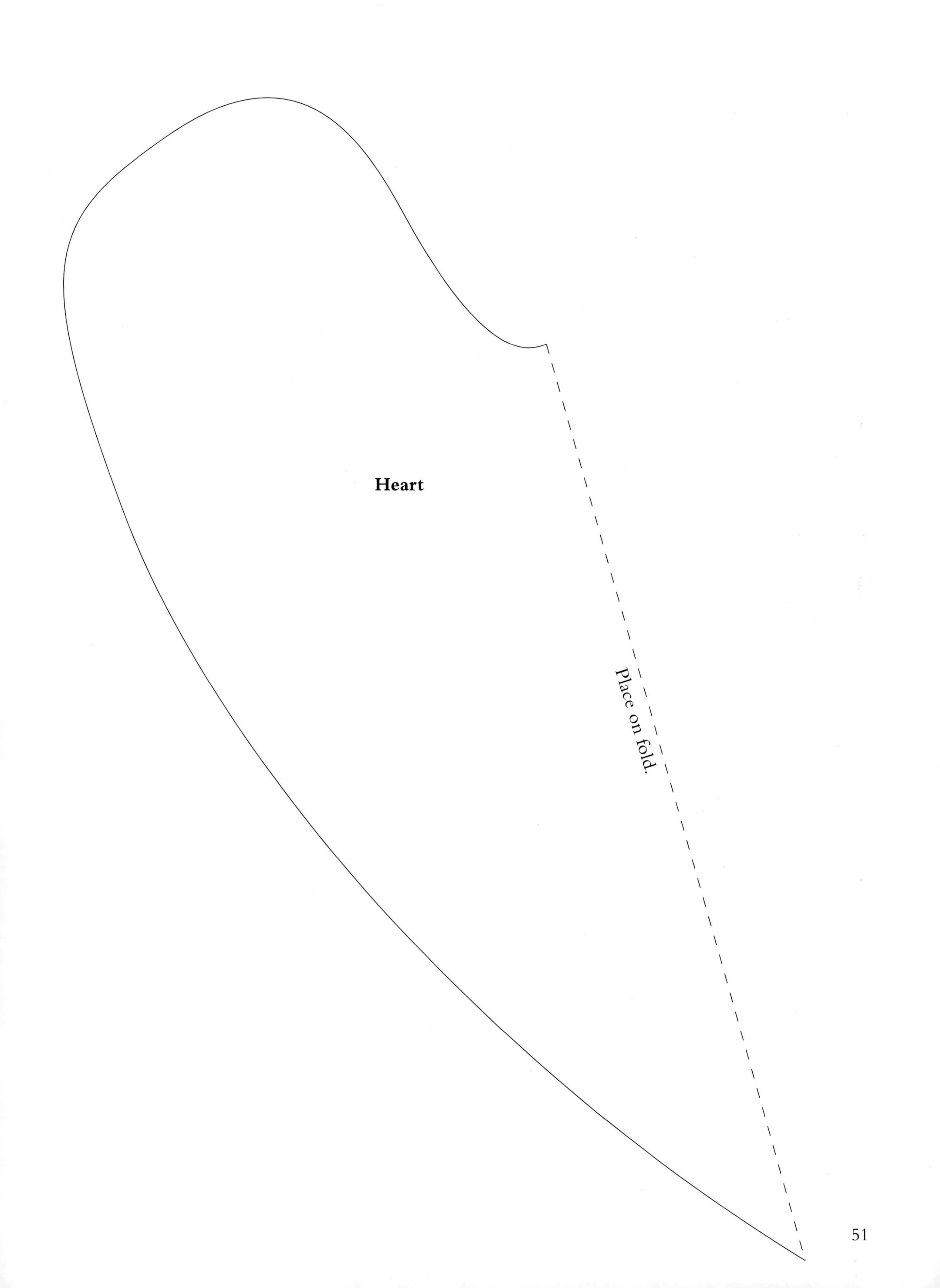
Heart
Place on fold.

Mother's Brag Book

Give Mom a keepsake album covered with fabric and embellished with buttons and lace.

Materials

- Photo album
- Craft fleece (See Step 1.)
- Fabric (See steps 1 and 3.)
- Aleene's Tacky Glue™
- Clothespins
- ½"-wide lace trim (See steps 2 and 4.)
- 1¼ yards ⅛"-wide ribbon to match fabric
- Posterboard (See Step 3.)
- Disappearing-ink pen
- Assorted buttons
- Satin cording with 1 tassel at each end

Directions

1 Open photo album and lay flat on top of fleece. Trace album cover and cut out 1 piece of fleece. Using fleece as guide, cut 1 piece of fabric, adding 1¼" all around. Glue fleece to cover outside of album cover. Center and glue album on wrong side of fabric. Fold excess fabric to inside of album cover and glue, mitering corners. Use clothespins to hold fabric in place until glue is dry.

2 Cut 1 piece of lace trim to fit around edge of opened album cover. Glue bound edge of lace trim around edge on inside of album cover so that lace extends beyond edge of album. Let dry. To make tie, cut ribbon in half. Fold each ribbon length in half. Center and glue fold of 1 ribbon on inside front cover at side edge. Repeat to glue remaining ribbon on inside back cover. Let dry.

3 For inside front cover, cut 1 piece of posterboard, ¼" smaller all around than inside front of album cover. Using posterboard piece as guide, cut 1 piece of fabric, adding 1¼" all around. Center and glue posterboard on wrong side of fabric. Fold excess fabric to back of posterboard and glue, mitering corners. With right side up, center and glue covered posterboard on inside front cover of album, covering fold of ribbon and bound edge of lace. Use clothespins to hold posterboard in place until glue is dry. In same manner, glue fabric-covered posterboard to inside back cover of album.

4 Center and draw heart shape on outside front cover of album, using disappearing-ink pen. (*Note:* See pages 39 and 63 for a selection of heart patterns.) Cut 1 piece of lace trim to fit perimeter of heart. Beginning at center top of heart, glue lace trim along marked line on album cover. Let dry. Glue buttons to cover area of heart (see photo). Let dry. Loop satin cording around spine of album and knot on outside of cover. Tie ribbons in bow.

Design by Hancock Fabrics

Romantic Bride's Gift

For a bridal shower gift, make this easy lace-trimmed padded hanger and a matching sachet.

Materials

For each: **Aleene's Tacky Glue™**
Assorted embellishments (See photos for inspiration.)

For 1 hanger: **Plastic or wooden V-shaped hanger**
¼"-wide ribbon: 1 (36") length, 1¼ yards, 1 (9") length
½ yard batting
¼ yard fabric
Thread to match
1½ yards pearl strand
1½ yards ¼"-wide lace trim or braid
2½ yards 2"- to 3"-wide lace
1¼ yards each 1½"-wide ribbon, ⅜"-wide ribbon

For 1 sachet: **6" x 9" piece fabric**
¼"-wide ribbon: 2 (9") lengths, ¾ yard
26" length 2"-wide lace
¾ yard each ⅞"-wide ribbon, ⅜"-wide ribbon
Stuffing
Potpourri

Directions for hanger

Note: Use ¼" seam allowance.

1 Apply glue to hook of hanger. Beginning at tip, wrap 36" ribbon length around hook, overlapping ribbon edges. Knot ribbon around hook at base and trim excess. Measure length of hanger. Cut 2 (4"-wide) pieces of batting to that measurement. Center and cut 1 hole for hanger hook in 1 piece of batting. Slip prepared batting over hanger hook. Place remaining batting piece on bottom of hanger. Overlap and glue long edges of batting pieces to cover hanger with batting. Let dry.

2 For hanger cover, measure around 1 arm of hanger. Add ½" to that measurement. Measure length of 1 arm of hanger from base of hook to end of hanger arm. Add ¾" to that measurement. Cut 2 hanger covers to these measurements, rounding 1 short end of each cover. With right sides facing and raw edges aligned, fold 1 hanger cover in half lengthwise. Stitch along long edge and curved end, leaving short straight end open. Clip curves and turn. Repeat with remaining hanger cover. With seam at bottom of hanger, slip 1 hanger cover over each arm of batting-covered hanger. Overlap raw ends where covers meet, turn under ¼" around edge of top cover, and glue to secure. Pin covers in place until glue is dry.

3 Measure around 1 arm of padded hanger. Referring to photo, cut 6 lengths each of pearl strand and/or ¼"-wide lace trim or braid to that measurement. Beginning and ending at seam on bottom of hanger, glue 3 lengths of pearl strand and/or lace trim or braid around each arm of hanger, spacing lengths evenly (see photo). Measure length of padded hanger. Multiply measurement by 2. Cut 2 lengths of lace to that measurement. Beginning and ending at center of hanger, glue 1 lace piece lengthwise around hanger, placing bound edge of

Designs by Hancock Fabrics

lace about 1" above bottom seam (see photo). In same manner, glue remaining lace piece around hanger, placing bound edge of lace about ¾" above edge of first lace piece.

4 Handling 1¼ yards of ¼"-wide ribbon, 1½"-wide ribbon, and ⅜"-wide ribbon as 1, make multilooped bow. Knot 9" length of ¼"-wide ribbon around center of bow to secure. To attach bow to hanger, knot ends of 9" ribbon around hanger hook at base.

5 Referring to photos for inspiration, glue assorted embellishments to hanger as desired.

Directions for sachet

1 Transfer pattern to fabric and cut 1 sachet. Fold 1 (9") ribbon length in half to form loop. Glue ribbon ends to wrong side of fabric where indicated on pattern. Let dry. Glue bound edge of lace around edge on right side of fabric so that lace extends beyond edge of fabric. Let dry.

2 With wrong sides facing, edges aligned, and ribbon hanger extending past edge of fabric, fold fabric in half along fold line. Glue fabric edges together, leaving opening for stuffing. Let dry. Stuff sachet with stuffing and potpourri. Glue opening closed. Handling ¾ yard of ¼"-wide ribbon, ⅞"-wide ribbon, and ⅜"-wide ribbon as 1, make multilooped bow. Knot remaining 9" length of ¼"-wide ribbon around center of bow to secure. To attach bow to sachet, knot ends of 9" ribbon around base of hanger loop at top of sachet.

3 Referring to photos for inspiration, glue assorted embellishments to sachet as desired.

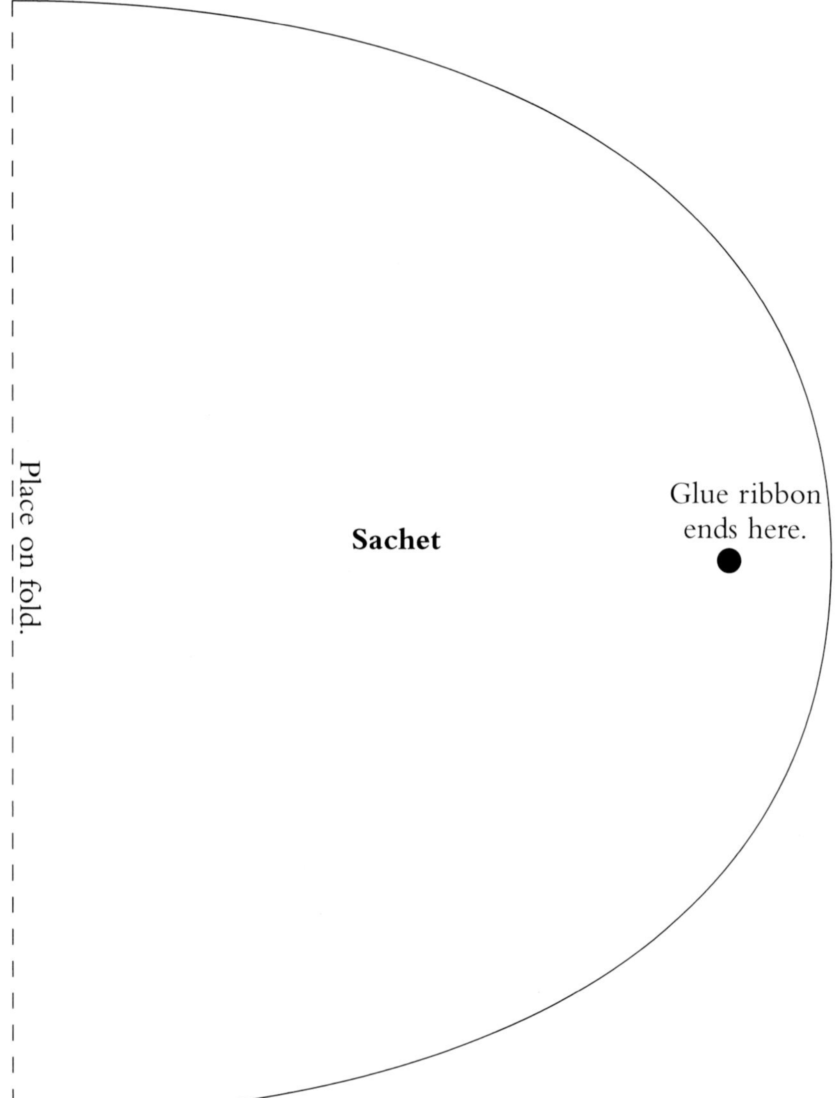

Shoe Shine

Preserve precious memories by applying a gold finish to a pair of baby shoes.

Materials

Delta Renaissance Foil: kit in desired color (base coat, adhesive, foil, antique, and sealer)
Pair of baby shoes
Paintbrush

Directions

1 Apply 1 coat of Renaissance sealer to entire surface of each shoe. Let dry. Paint each shoe with Renaissance base coat. Let dry. Apply 1 coat of Renaissance adhesive to each shoe. Let dry until clear. To apply foil, lay foil dull side down on top of adhesive-covered area. Using finger, press foil onto adhesive. Peel away foil paper. If any part of adhesive is not covered, reapply foil as needed.

2 Brush Renaissance antique on each shoe. Wipe off excess with paper towel. Let dry. Apply 1 coat of Renaissance sealer to each shoe. Let dry.

Design by Joyce Bennett, SCD, CCD, CPD/ Delta Technical Coatings

Sensational Satin

Designs by Mary Holman Allen/ Sew Easy Textiles, Inc.

Bridal Bag

Materials

For angel bear: **⅔ yard 6½"-wide Sew Easy Textiles Satin Basket Trim**
8" high plush bear
Poly-fil® stuffing
Aleene's Designer Tacky Glue™ and low-temp hot-glue glue and glue sticks (See note.)
½ yard 2"-wide Sew Easy Textiles Gold Metallic Lace Ruffle
4"-wide white-and-gold wings
1 gold glitter chenille stem
⅔ yard Sew Easy Textiles Iridescent Pearl strand (4-mm diameter)
Offray gold ribbon rose

For bridal bag: **⅔ yard 3"-wide lace with floral motif**
Aleene's Jewel-It™ Glue
3"-diameter cardboard circle
1 yard 6½"-wide Sew Easy Textiles Satin Basket Trim
Waxed paper
Iridescent sequins and pearls
Small safety pin
¾ yard ¼"-diameter white-and-gold cording

For ring bearer pillow: **Aleene's Designer Tacky Glue™ and low-temp hot-glue gun and glue sticks (See note.)**
2 (30") lengths Sew Easy Textiles Bridal Satin Basket Trim
10"-diameter round pillow form
30" length Sew Easy Textiles Lace-Edged Basket Handle Trim
2 yards 1"-wide Sew Easy Textiles Iridescent Ribbon (MFL)
White florist's wire
2 artificial wedding rings
Assorted white silk flowers
Pearl sprays

Delight a bride with these white satin keepsake wedding accessories.

Directions for angel bear

Note: To use Designer Tacky Glue in combination with glue gun, apply small amounts of each glue for strong and permanent bond.

1 Pull both bottom wires of Satin Basket Trim to gather around top of bear's legs. Secure wire ends and trim excess wire. Pull both top wires of Satin Basket Trim to gather around bear's neck, placing stuffing inside fabric around bear's body. Secure wire ends and trim excess wire. Overlap ends of Satin Basket Trim at back of bear. Cut slits in fabric for bear's arms.

2 Glue Lace Ruffle around bear's neck. Let dry. Glue wings to back of bear. Curve chenille stem into circle for halo, twisting chenille ends together to secure. Wrap pearl strand around halo, gluing ends of strand to secure. Trim excess pearl strand. Glue halo to back of bear's head. Let dry. Wrap remaining pearl strand around bear's neck with streamers at front and glue to secure. Glue ribbon rose to bear at neck. Let dry.

Directions for bridal bag

1 Cut 2 (3"-diameter) circles from lace. Glue 1 circle to each side of cardboard circle. Let dry. Cut desired motifs from

Angel Bear

remaining lace. Lay Satin Basket Trim flat on work surface covered with waxed paper. Glue desired lace motifs in place on Satin Basket Trim. Glue sequins and pearls on each lace motif. Let dry.

2 Pull topmost wire on Satin Basket Trim to remove from casing. Attach safety pin to 1 end of cording. Using safety pin as bodkin, thread cording through top casing on Satin Basket Trim. Pull both bottom wires on Satin Basket Trim to gather for bottom of bag. Secure wire ends and trim excess wire. Place lace-covered cardboard in bottom of bag. Overlap ends of Satin Basket Trim and glue to secure. Let dry. Pull cording and knot ends to close bag.

Directions for pillow

Note: To use Designer Tacky Glue in combination with glue gun, apply small amounts of each glue for strong and permanent bond.

1 For bottom of pillow, with bottom wire aligned with seam of pillow form, glue 1 (30") length of Satin Basket Trim around edge of pillow. Overlap ends of Satin Basket Trim, turn top end under ¼", and glue to secure. Let dry. Pull both top wires on Satin Basket Trim to gather tightly to cover bottom of pillow, turning ruffle under. In same manner, glue remaining 30" length of Satin Basket Trim around pillow for top of pillow. Let dry. Gather Satin Basket Trim to cover top of pillow but do not turn ruffle under. Glue Handle Trim around edge of pillow to cover glued seam. Let dry.

2 Cut ribbon in half. Make multilooped bow with 1 yard of ribbon. Secure bow with florist's wire. Glue bow to top of pillow near ruffle. Let dry. Cut remaining yard of ribbon in half. Tie each ribbon length in bow. Glue 1 bow to top of pillow on each side of multilooped bow. Let dry. Tie wedding rings to bow streamers or glue to top of pillow as desired. Glue silk flowers and pearl sprays to pillow as desired. Let dry.

Ring Bearer Pillow

Design by Marlene Watson, SCD/House of Fabrics

Treasure Chest

Apply fabric cutouts to a wooden box. Outline the cutouts with lines of gold foil for an elegant touch.

Materials

Wooden box
Sandpaper
½" flat shader paintbrush
Aleene's Premium-Coat™ Acrylic Paint: Deep Blue (or color to match fabric)
Print fabric scraps
Aleene's Paper Napkin Appliqué™ Glue
Aleene's Gloss Right-On Finish™
Aleene's 3-D Foiling™ Glue
Aleene's Gold Crafting Foil™

Directions

1 Sand box. Paint box with 2 coats of paint, letting dry between coats. Cut desired motifs from print fabric scraps. To apply each cutout to box, brush coat of Napkin Appliqué Glue on box in desired position. Press fabric cutout into glue. Brush coat of Napkin Appliqué Glue on top of cutout, pressing out any air bubbles. Brush coat of Napkin Appliqué Glue over entire surface of box. Let dry. Apply 1 coat of finish to box. Let dry.

2 Outline fabric cutouts and add details with 3-D Foiling Glue. Let dry. (Glue will be opaque and sticky when dry. Glue must be thoroughly dry before foil is applied.) To apply gold foil, lay foil dull side down on top of glue design. Using finger, gently but firmly press foil onto glue, completely covering glue with foil. Peel away foil paper. If any part of glue is not covered, reapply foil as needed.

*Design by Rebecca Hermann/
Jo-Ann Fabrics and Crafts*

HEARTS & PATCHES

Materials

Rotary cutter with pinking blade
June Tailor Cutting and Pinweaving Board
Fabrics: blue floral print, pink floral print, pink, blue heart-and-floral print, blue
Aleene's Fusible Web™
12" square Warm and Natural Batting
Pearl cotton thread: blue, pink
14 (3") lengths each ⅜"-wide satin ribbon: pink, blue
Aleene's Tacky Glue™
3" length ¼"-wide lace trim

Use a rotary cutter with a pinking blade to give a decorative edge to the fabrics in this tiny quilt.

Directions

Note: See page 5 for tips on working with fusible web.

1 Using rotary cutter with pinking blade and cutting board, cut 2 (12") squares from blue floral, 1 (6") square and 4 (3") squares from pink floral, and 12 (1½" x 2") pieces from pink. Using scissors, transfer pattern and cut 1 large heart section from pink, 4 small hearts from blue heart-and-floral, and 1 entire large heart from blue. Using scissors, cut 4 (3"-diameter) circles from blue heart-and-floral. Fuse web on wrong side of each piece except 12" squares and 3" circles. Referring to photo for placement, fuse 6" pink floral square, 3" pink floral squares, 1½" x 2" pink pieces, and small blue heart-and-floral hearts on right side of 1 (12") blue floral square.

2 Stack remaining blue floral square (right side down), batting, and fused blue floral square (right side up). Whipstitch layers together, using blue pearl cotton thread.

3 With right side down, pin blue ribbon lengths side by side on board. Beginning at bottom of blue lengths and working with right sides down, weave pink lengths through blue lengths. Be sure resulting fabric will not have gaps between woven lengths. Fuse web onto woven ribbon fabric. Transfer pattern to woven fabric and cut 1 large heart woven section.

Referring to pattern, fuse woven section and large heart pink section in place on large blue heart. Fuse large heart on quilt. Referring to photo, do decorative stitching on quilt with pearl cotton thread.

4 For yo-yos, run pearl cotton gathering thread around each fabric circle ¼" from edge. Pull tightly to gather circle into yo-yo and secure thread. Glue yo-yos and lace trim to large heart, trimming lace to fit as needed. Let dry.

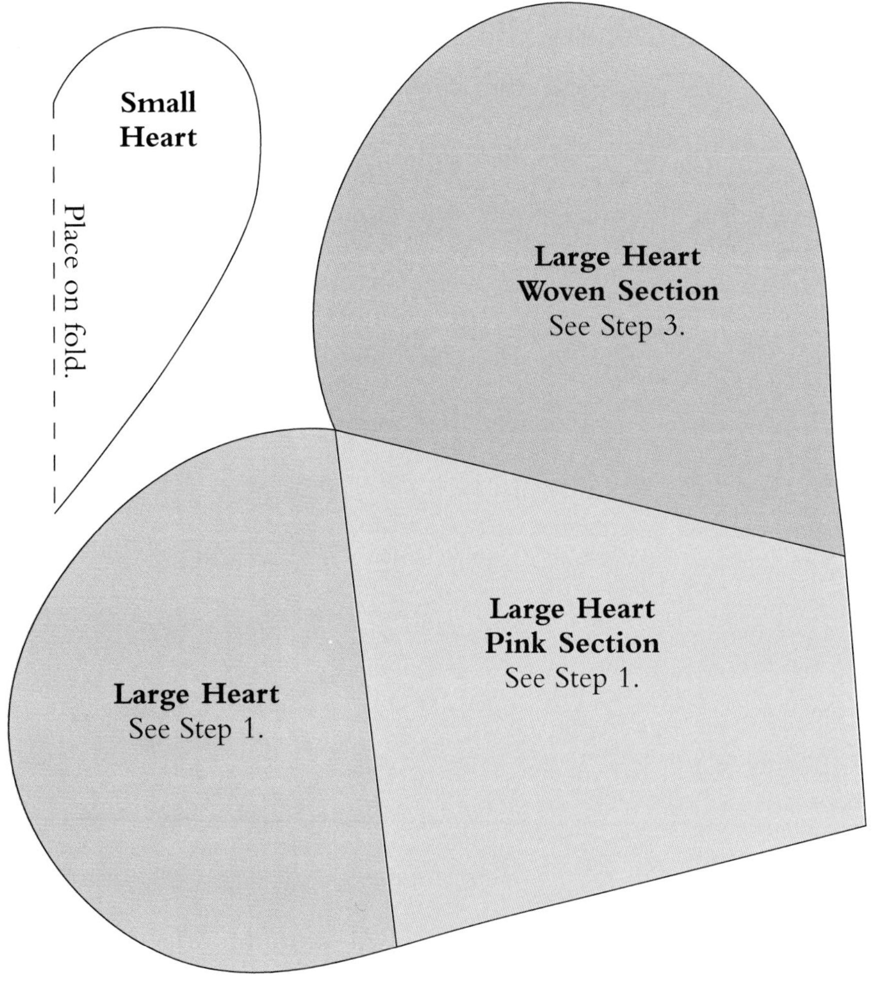

Painting *Miss Daisy*

Paint wooden cutouts and pair them with buttons to decorate frames and flowerpots.

Materials

For each: **Frame, flowerpot, or box**
Wooden cutouts: 3"-diameter flower, 1⅜"-diameter circle, ¼" x 5" strip, 1¼"-long leaf (See note.)
Aleene's Enhancers™ All-Purpose Primer
Sponge paintbrush
Sandpaper
Aleene's Premium-Coat™ Acrylic Paints: White, Light Blue, assorted colors for wooden cutouts
¾"-wide masking tape
Natural sea sponge
Assorted buttons
Aleene's Designer Tacky Glue™
Ribbon scrap (optional)

Directions

Note: If desired, cut shapes from posterboard or lightweight cardboard instead of using wooden cutouts.

1 Apply 1 coat of primer to base piece and each wooden cutout. Let dry. Lightly sand wooden pieces. Paint base piece

with 1 or 2 coats of White, letting dry between coats. For lattice design, press lengths of masking tape onto base piece, spacing tape lengths about 1¼" apart (see photo). Be sure edges of tape securely adhere to base piece to keep paint from seeping underneath. Dip dampened sea sponge into Light Blue paint and sponge-paint base piece as desired. Let dry. Remove tape.

2 Paint wooden cutouts with desired colors of paint. Let dry. Referring to photo for inspiration, glue cutouts and buttons onto base piece as desired. Let dry. If desired, knot center of ribbon or tie ribbon in bow. Glue ribbon or bow onto base piece.

Designs by Inga Johns/Duncan Enterprises

Gone Fishin'

For a unique Father's Day gift, make fish from bread dough and string them on leather cord.

Materials
6 slices white bread with crusts removed
Plastic bowl
Aleene's Tacky Glue™
Wooden craft stick
Zip-top plastic bag
Hot-glue gun mat or waxed paper
1 grommet in size to fit each fish
Foam meat tray, washed and dried
Assorted colors Aleene's Premium-Coat™ Acrylic Paints
Paintbrush
Toothbrush
Leather cord

Directions

1 To make bread dough, tear bread into small pieces and put pieces in plastic bowl. Add 6 tablespoons glue to bread and mix with craft stick until coarse ball forms. Remove ball of dough from bowl. With clean hands, knead dough for about 5 minutes or until it is smooth and pliable. If dough is too coarse, add a little more glue. Dough will stick to your hands until it becomes smooth. Place dough in zip-top bag when not in use.

2 Place patterns (on page 68) under hot-glue gun mat or waxed paper. Pinch off ball of dough for each fish. Press dough onto mat with fingers to about 1/4" thick, shaping dough to fit pattern. For eye, dip 1/2 of grommet into glue and push into fish.

Design by Hancock Fabrics

Carefully peel fish from mat. Remove dough from eye center. Dip remaining ½ of grommet into glue and attach to grommet in fish. Referring to photo, press ridges into tail on both sides of fish, using fingers. Lay fish flat on mat and let dry for about 24 hours, turning several times during drying.

3 Referring to photo, paint both sides of each fish desired base color. Paint gill line on each side of each fish with desired contrasting color. To spatter-paint each fish, dip toothbrush into desired color of paint. With bristles pointing toward fish, rub finger across bristles to spatter fish with paint. Repeat to spatter each fish with 2 or 3 colors of paint. Let dry.

4 Cut leather cord to desired length for each fish. Knot 1 length of cord to eye of each fish. Knot free ends of cord together.

Frame Weaving

Luxurious yarn makes this plastic canvas frame extra-special.

Materials

- 3⅞" x 5¼" piece 14-mesh plastic canvas (14 holes per inch)
- 1 spool Bond America Multi's Embellishment Yarn: Willow Rose
- Large-eyed tapestry needle
- 3" x 5" acrylic frame
- Aleene's Designer Tacky Glue™

Directions

Mark rectangle on plastic canvas 1" from all edges. Cut out marked rectangle. Set cutout aside for another use. Referring to photo, work tent stitch over 13-mesh square in each corner of frame. Work overcast stitch around inner and outer edges of frame. Referring to Diagram and photo, work long stitch over remaining areas of frame to make zigzag pattern. Be sure to cut new yarn length beginning with ending shade to maintain color sequence. Glue stitched frame onto acrylic frame. Let dry.

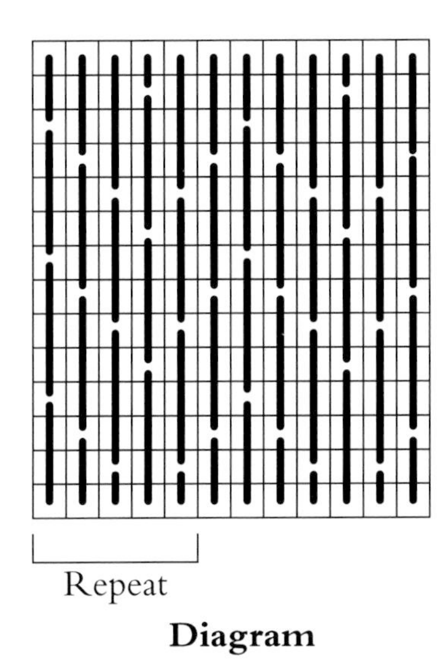

Diagram

Design by Cari Clement/Bond America

Lace & Elegance

Present each of your wedding attendants with a pretty memory box.

Materials

For each: **Darice round papier-mâché box**
Textured fabric in desired color or Foreston Trends Traditions Cloth Napkin (See note.)
1 Banar Stick 'n Puff heart
Desired color Aleene's Premium-Coat™ Acrylic Paint
Paintbrush
Aleene's Designer Tacky Glue™
Sculptured bridal lace
½"-wide braided trim
1 Catan Wedding Floral Strand
12" length satin cording
Pearl strands

Directions for 1 box

Note: You may need more than 1 napkin depending on size of papier-mâché box.

1 Measure height and circumference of box sides. Add 1" to measurements and cut strip of fabric to match. Trace lid onto fabric, adding 1" all around. Cut out fabric for lid. Following manufacturer's directions, cover Stick 'n Puff heart with fabric.

2 Paint inside of box and lid. Let dry. Paint bottom of box. Let dry. With 1 long edge of fabric strip aligned with bottom of box, glue fabric strip around sides of box. Overlap ends of fabric, turn top end under ¼", and glue. Fold excess fabric over top edge of box and glue. Spread glue on top and sides of lid. Center and place lid, glue side down, on wrong side of lid fabric. Press fabric into glue, trimming excess fabric from edge of lid. Let dry.

3 Place lid on box. With bound edge of lace aligned with bottom edge of lid, glue sculptured lace around sides of box (see photo). Glue braided trim around edge of heart. Center and glue heart on lid. Referring to photo for inspiration, glue remaining braided trim, Wedding Floral Strand, satin cording, and pearl strands to box and lid as desired. Let dry.

Designs by Violet Lynn/Old America Stores

the Kitchen Of

Red Hot Chili Peppers

Use a chili pepper stencil to make package tie-ons for bottles of flavored vinegar.

Materials

For each: **Stencil paintbrushes: 1/8"-wide, 1/4"-wide**
Stencil paints: red, yellow, green
White paper
American Traditional Stencil: Chili Pepper (#MS-156) and Vegetable "From the Kitchen" (FS-905)

For bag: **Small muslin bag**
Lightweight cardboard scrap

For gift tag: **2½" x 3" piece watercolor paper**
Decorative-blade scissors (optional)

For pin: **Aleene's Opake Shrink-It™ Plastic**
Decorative-blade scissors (optional)
Aleene's Baking Board or nonstick cookie sheet, sprinkled with baby powder
Aleene's Tacky Glue™
Pin back

Directions

To stencil design, put tiny dot of 1 color of paint on tip of brush. Rub brush in circular motion on white paper to distribute paint on brush. Tap brush on desired area of stencil. Repeat to stencil entire design, using colors as desired. For shaded effect, tap brush around edge of stencil area to apply more paint to edges of design. Let dry. Remove stencil.

For bag, place scrap of cardboard inside bag. Position stencil on bag and tape to secure. Stencil design on bag.

For gift tag, fold watercolor paper in half widthwise to form gift tag. If desired, cut edge of card with decorative-blade scissors (see photo). Position stencil on front of tag and tape to secure. Stencil design on tag.

For pin, position stencil on Shrink-It and tape to secure. Stencil design on Shrink-It. Cut out stenciled design, leaving 1/4"-wide border around design. If desired, trim edge of cutout with decorative-blade scissors.

Preheat toaster oven or conventional oven to 275° to 300°. Place design on room-temperature baking board and bake in oven. Edges should begin to curl within 25 seconds; if not, increase temperature slightly. If edges begin to curl as soon as design is put in oven, reduce temperature. After about 1 minute, design will lie flat. Remove from oven. Let cool. Center and glue pin back to wrong side of design. Let dry.

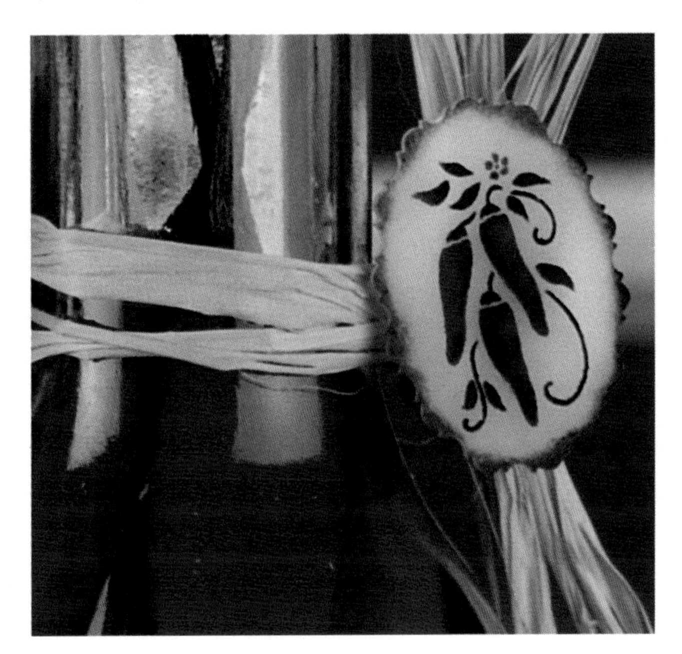

Design by Judith Barker/American Traditional Stencils

Fashion

Use the simple techniques in this chapter to turn T-shirts, sweatshirts, and other purchased garments into wearable art.

Page 82

Page 76

Page 100

Page 89

Page 92

HOME IS WHERE THE HEART IS

Sunflower Sweatshirt

Stitch a collar and pockets onto a sweatshirt. Add crow and sunflower appliqués to create this must-have cardigan.

Materials

Fabrics: 1 yard brown plaid, ½ yard yellow print, green print scrap, black scrap, white-on-white print scrap
Threads: white, gold
Aleene's Fusible Web™
1 yard tear-away stabilizer
White Jerzee's sweatshirt
Fusible interfacing
7 sunflower buttons
Aleene's OK to Wash-It™ Glue (optional)
Assorted brown buttons

Directions

Note: Patterns on pages 78–81. Use ¼" seam allowance.

See page 5 for tips on working with fusible web.

See page 50 for directions for stuffed fabric heart.

1 Transfer patterns to brown plaid and cut 2 collars and 4 pockets. With right sides facing and raw edges aligned, stitch collar pieces together, leaving opening. Clip curves and turn. Turn under ¼" along opening and slipstitch opening closed. In same manner, stitch pieces together to make 2 pockets.

2 Fuse web to wrong side of remaining fabrics. Transfer patterns to fabrics and cut 4 large centers, 4 medium centers, and 6 small centers from brown plaid; 4 large flowers, 4 medium flowers, and 6 small flowers from yellow print; 7 leaf As, 4 leaf Bs, 1 stem A, and 1 stem B from green print; 1 bird and 1 wing from black; and 2 crossbars from white-on-white print. Reverse patterns and cut 1 bird and 1 wing from remaining black. Also cut 2 (⅞" x 7") strips and 1 (⅞" x 6⅜") strip from remaining white-on-white print for fence posts. Cut 1 end of each post to form point.

3 Referring to diagrams, arrange appliqués on each pocket and on collar. For appliqués that extend beyond edges of base piece, transfer patterns to fabrics and cut pieces from remaining fabrics for back of extended area of appliqué. Fuse pieces to backs of appliqués as needed. Fuse appliqués in place on each pocket and on collar. Pin tear-away stabilizer to wrong side of each pocket and collar. Machine-appliqué designs using white thread for fence pieces and gold thread for all other pieces. Remove stabilizer.

4 To find center front of shirt, fold shirt in half lengthwise, aligning shoulders and side seams. Press along fold. Unfold shirt. Cut along fold line. Cut off ribbing at neckline. Mark center back of shirt at neckline. Beginning and ending 5" from center front opening, run gathering thread along neckline of shirt. Pull thread to slightly gather shirt.

5 With edges aligned, pin collar right side up on right side of shirt, matching center back of collar to marked point on shirt. Match Xs on collar to beginning and ending points of gathering stitches, adjusting gathers to fit. Be sure points of collar are even at front of shirt. Stitch collar to shirt. Trim top front corners from shirt. Measure around neckline along edge of collar. Cut 1 (1½"-wide) strip of brown plaid fabric to that measurement. Turn under ¼" along each long edge of strip and press. Fold strip in half lengthwise and press. Stitch strip around neckline to bind collar.

6 Measure length of 1 edge at front opening of shirt. Add 1" to that measurement. Cut 2 (2¼"-wide) strips of brown plaid to this measurement. Fuse interfacing to wrong side of each strip. Turn under ¼" along each long edge of each strip and press. Fold each strip in half lengthwise and press. Stitch 1 strip to each front edge of shirt, allowing strip to extend ½" beyond top and bottom of shirt. Turn under excess fabric at top and bottom of strip and stitch. Make 7 buttonholes evenly spaced along left-hand edge of shirt. Stitch sunflower buttons along right-hand edge of shirt. Referring to photo, stitch pockets in place on shirt, leaving 6" opening at top for hand. Glue or stitch 1 brown button in place for eye on each bird. Glue or stitch assorted brown buttons in place on flower centers and fence as desired. Let glue dry.

Design by Rebecca Hermann/Jo-Ann Fabrics and Crafts

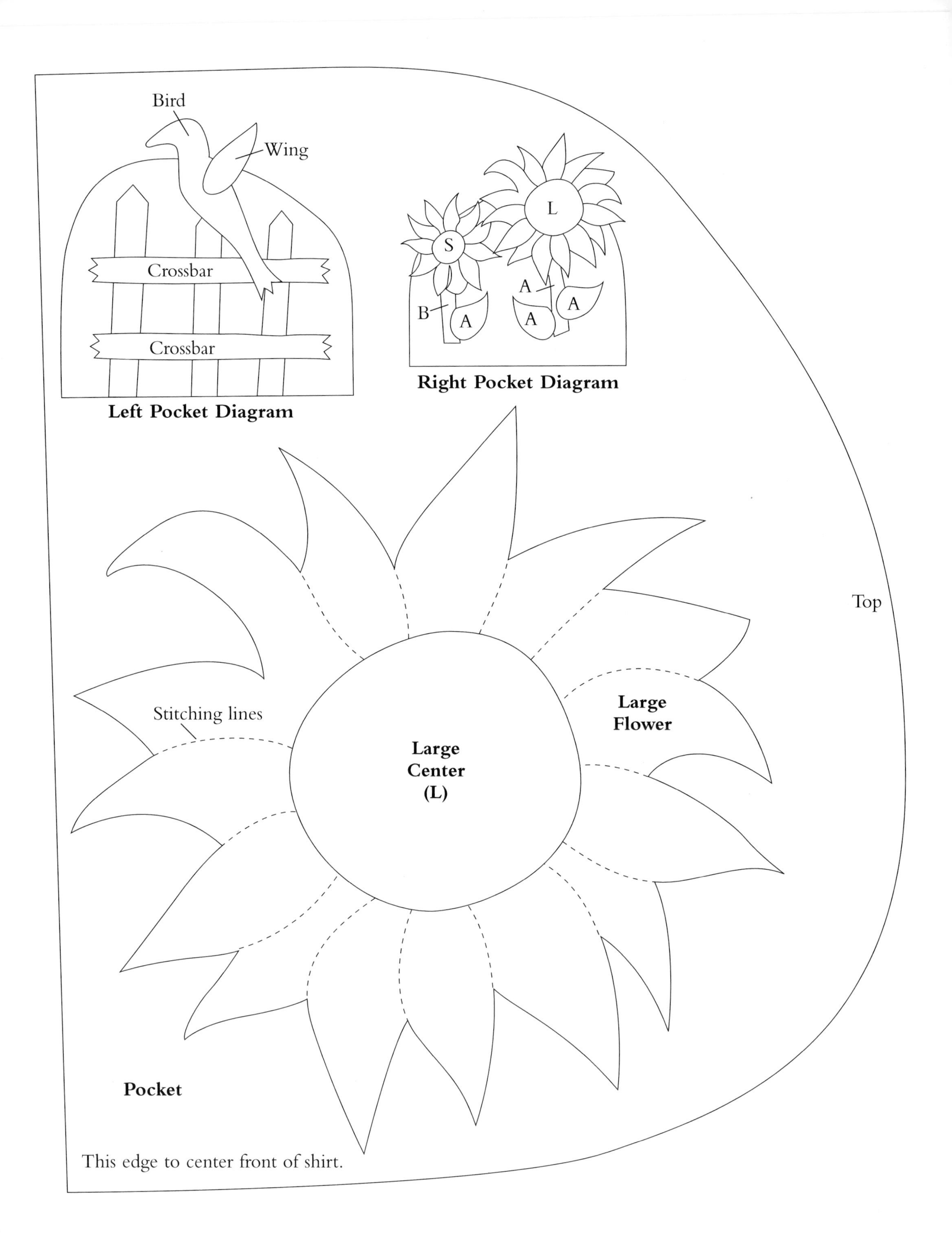

Bird
Wing
Crossbar
Crossbar
Left Pocket Diagram
L
S
A
A
B
A
A
Right Pocket Diagram
Top
Stitching lines
Large Flower
Large Center (L)
Pocket
This edge to center front of shirt.

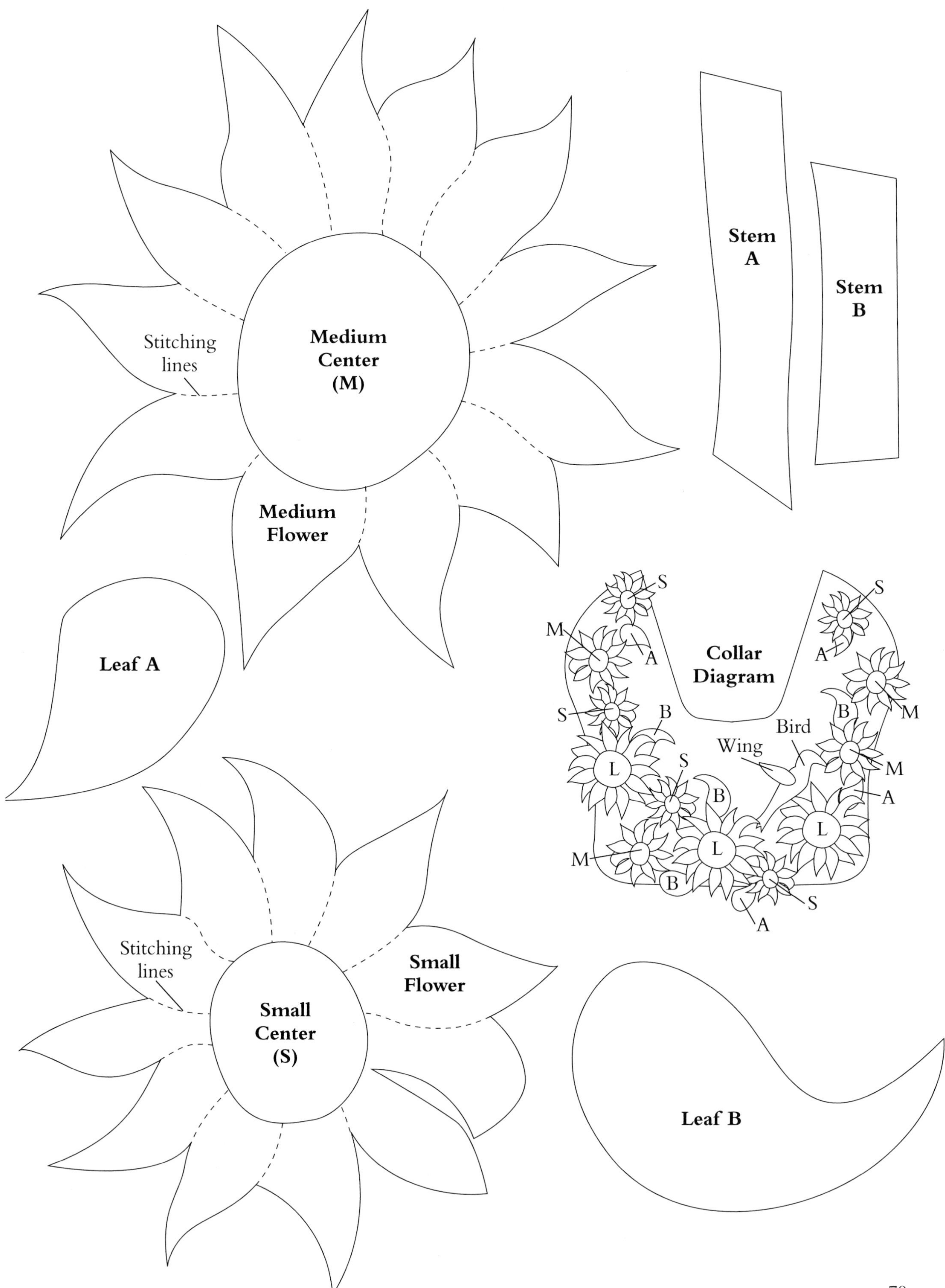
Medium Center (M)
Medium Flower
Stitching lines
Stem A
Stem B
Leaf A
Collar Diagram
S
M
A
B
L
Bird
Wing
Small Flower
Small Center (S)
Stitching lines
Leaf B

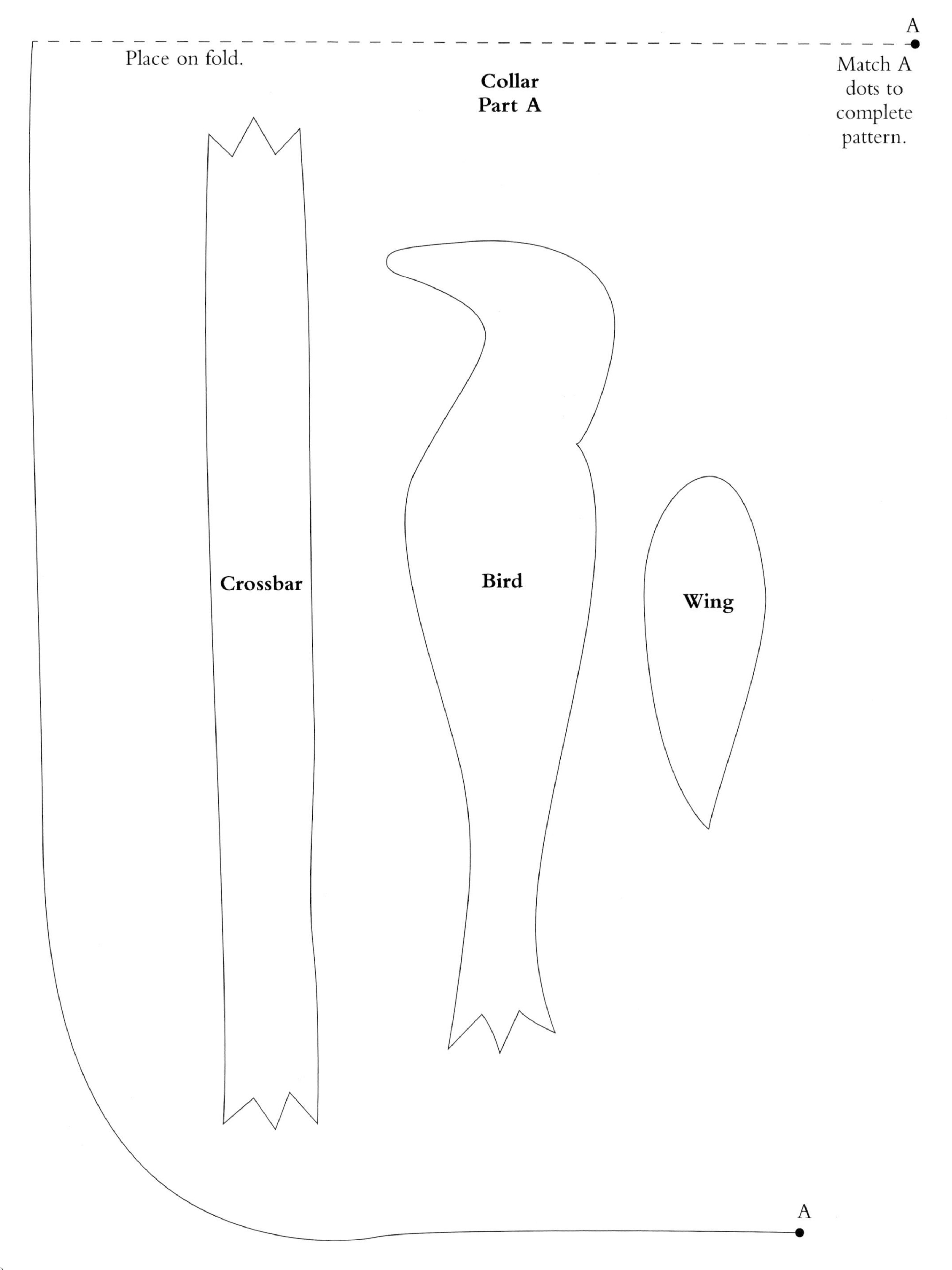
A
Place on fold.
Collar
Part A
Match A
dots to
complete
pattern.
Crossbar
Bird
Wing
A

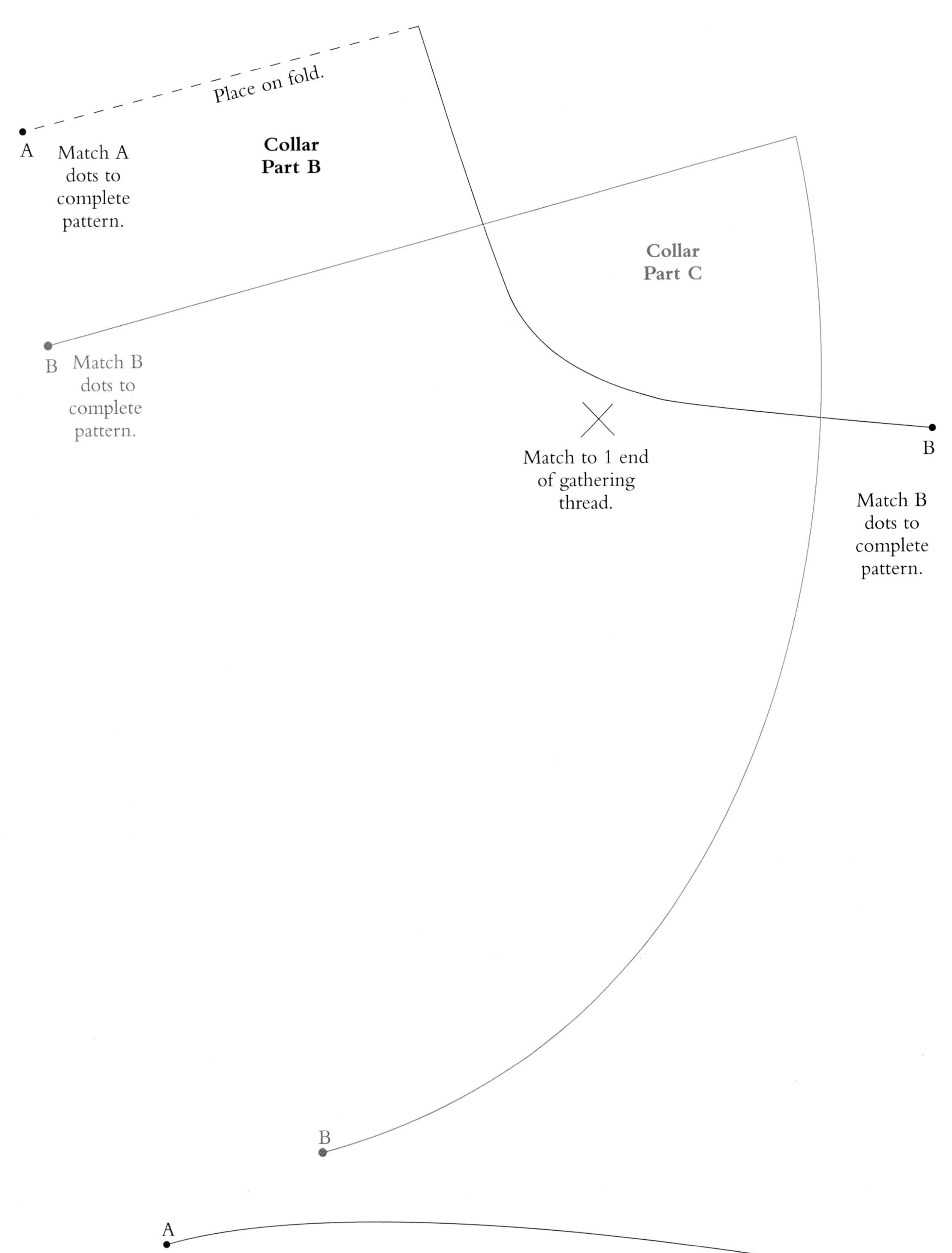
Place on fold.
A
Match A dots to complete pattern.
Collar Part B
Collar Part C
B
Match B dots to complete pattern.
Match to 1 end of gathering thread.
B
Match B dots to complete pattern.
B
A
B

Painted Roses Outfit

Use pieces cut from a washcloth to paint roses and leaves on a shirt and boxer shorts.

Materials

- White T-shirt
- White boxer shorts
- White washcloth
- Cardboard covered with waxed paper
- 3 rubber bands
- Aleene's Enhancers™ Textile Medium
- Aleene's Premium-Coat™ Acrylic Paints: Medium Fuchsia, Medium Green, White, Medium Violet
- Pencil with eraser
- Aleene's OK to Wash-It™ Glue
- Crystal glitter
- Pearl dimensional paint

Directions

1 Wash and dry shirt, boxer shorts, and washcloth; do not use fabric softener in washer or dryer. Place cardboard covered with waxed paper inside shirt and boxer shorts.

2 Cut washcloth in half. For rose, fold 1 washcloth piece in half lengthwise. Roll washcloth jellyroll fashion. Secure rolled piece with 1 rubber band placed near cut end. Cut remaining washcloth piece in half. For leaf, fold 1 washcloth piece in half widthwise. Fold in side edges to form triangle. Place thumb in center of triangle with base of triangle toward hand. Referring to photo, pull washcloth up around thumb and secure with 1 rubber band. Carefully remove thumb.

3 For each color of acrylic paint, mix equal parts textile medium and paint. Dip folded end of rose washcloth into Medium Fuchsia. Gently press washcloth on shirt to paint 1 rose. Move washcloth to another position and gently press on shirt to paint second rose. Repeat to paint additional roses on shirt and shorts as desired, dipping washcloth into paint as needed. Let dry. In same manner, paint leaves on shirt and shorts as desired, using leaf washcloth. Use full-strength Medium Green paint for some leaves. For remaining leaves, mix Medium Green and White paints. Let dry.

4 Dip pencil eraser into Medium Violet to paint dots on shirt and shorts as desired. Let dry. Fold remaining washcloth piece as for leaf piece and secure with remaining rubber band. Dip washcloth into glue and pounce on shirt and shorts around painted design. Sprinkle glitter onto wet glue. Let dry.

5 Embellish painted designs with dimensional paint as desired. Let dry. Do not wash shirt and shorts for at least 2 weeks. Turn shirt and shorts wrong side out, wash by hand, and hang to dry.

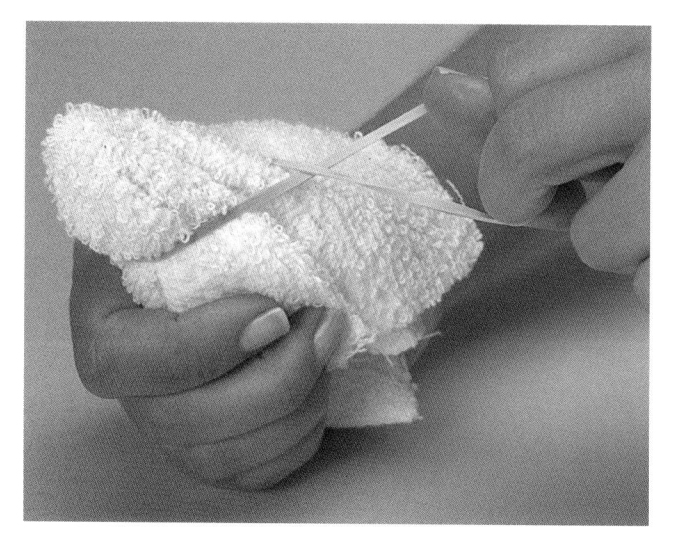

Wrap a piece of a washcloth around your thumb and secure it with a rubberband. Remove your thumb and use the prepared washcloth to paint the leaves on the garments.

Designs by Tracia Ledford, SCD, CPD, and Katelyn Ledford

VICTORIAN VEST

Glue crocheted place mats together to make this fashion accent.

Design by Old America Stores

Materials

Waxed paper
4 (12" x 18") crocheted place mats
Aleene's OK to Wash-It™ Glue
Paintbrush
3 small buttons
Thread to match place mat
3 decorative button covers

Directions

1 Cover work surface with waxed paper. Referring to Diagram, lay 4 mats right side down and side by side on covered work surface, overlapping long edges. Glue together overlapped edges of 2 center mats for back of vest. Glue together about 10" or 11" along overlapped edges of remaining mats for left front and right front of vest, leaving top 7" or 8" free for armholes. Let dry.

2 Fold left front and right front over back of vest. Slip 1 piece of waxed paper between front and back of vest at each armhole. With right front of vest overlapping back of vest, glue together about 6" or 8" from top of armhole toward center front along overlapped edges for shoulder seam. Repeat for left shoulder seam. Let dry.

3 Fold over each edge of vest opening from shoulder seam to desired length for lapels (see photo). Glue lapels in place. Let dry. Turn vest over. Fold down edge along back neckline of vest and glue for collar. Let dry.

4 Turn vest right side up. Stitch small buttons evenly spaced along left front of vest. Slip buttons through crocheted design at right front of vest to wear vest. Put covers on buttons after vest is fastened.

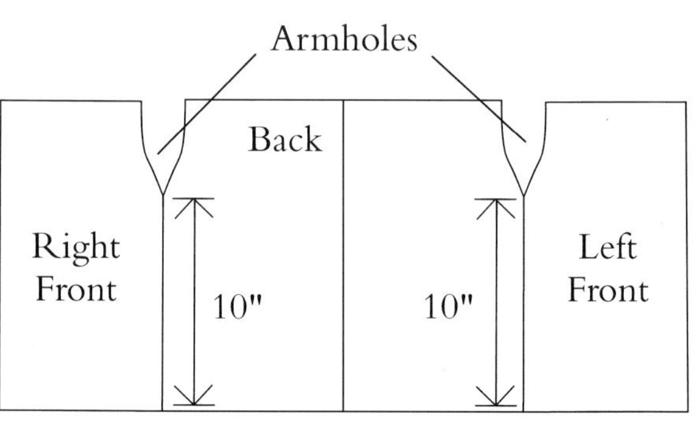

Diagram

Napkin Appliqué Casuals

Dress up a shirt and pants outfit with motifs cut from paper napkins.

Materials

Shirt and pants outfit
Cardboard covered with waxed paper
Waxed paper
Print paper napkins
Chalk pencil
½" flat shader paintbrush
Aleene's Paper Napkin Appliqué™ Glue
Dimensional paint to match paper napkin

Directions

1 Wash and dry shirt and pants; do not use fabric softener in washer or dryer. Place cardboard covered with waxed paper inside shirt. Place 1 piece of waxed paper inside pants leg where napkins will be glued.

2 Cut motifs from napkins as desired. Remove bottom plies of napkins to leave cutouts 1-ply thick. Place napkin cutouts on garments as desired. Trace around each napkin cutout, using chalk pencil. Working with 1 napkin cutout at a time, remove cutout from garment. Brush coat of glue on garment inside marked line. Press cutout into glue. Gently brush top of cutout with coat of glue. Be sure to completly seal cutout with glue. Repeat to apply additional cutouts to shirt and pants leg as desired. Let dry.

3 Outline and embellish cutouts with dimensional paint. Let dry. Do not wash shirt and pants for at least 1 week. Turn shirt and pants wrong side out, wash by hand, and hang to dry.

Design by Heidi Borchers, SCD/Aleene's

Country Angel Overalls

Paint an angel on white fabric that has been fused onto a purchased garment.

Materials

8" x 10" piece white 100% cotton fabric
Denim overalls
Photocopy of pattern on page 88
Aleene's Fusible Web™
Duncan Scribbles 3-Dimensional Fabric Writers: White (SC110), Black (SC139), Bright Red (SC121), Copper (SC226), Bright Green (SC134), Christmas Red (SC144), Glittering Gold (SC302)
Duncan Scribbles Brush 'n Soft Fabric Paint: Pink Surprise (FS143), Bright Orange (FS115), Deep Turquoise (FS131), Lemon Yellow (FS111)
Duncan Compliments Ultra Glitter Fabric Paint: Ruby (CU107), Gold (CU120)
Paintbrushes: #5 round soft-bristle, fine-tip
6" length ¼"-wide red-and-green plaid ribbon
Aleene's OK to Wash-It™ Glue

Directions

Note: See page 5 for tips on working with fusible web.

1 Wash white fabric and overalls; do not use fabric softener in washer or dryer. Center and pin photocopy of pattern facedown on fabric. Iron paper to transfer pattern to fabric. Remove paper.

2 Fuse web to wrong side of white fabric. Cut out angel and star. Fuse designs on front of overalls. Paint designs on fused fabric, using colors as follows and letting dry between colors. Use paint directly from Fabric Writer bottle to outline painted areas and add details.

To paint face and hand, mix White with Pink Surprise and small amount of Bright Orange. For shading on face and hand, mix White with Pink Surprise and small amount of Bright Orange, adding less White to mixture.

Paint cheeks and nose Pink Surprise.

Paint eyes Black.

To paint mouth, mix Pink Surprise and Bright Red. Use fine-tip brush to apply paint.

Paint hair Copper.

Paint dress Bright Green. For shading on dress, use Deep Turquoise. Paint trim on dress Lemon Yellow and Bright Red (see photo). Paint petticoat White. Add details to dress trim and paint dots on dress White.

Paint apron Bright Red. For shading on apron, use Christmas Red. Paint pocket on apron White. Paint heart on pocket Ruby. Paint trim on pocket Bright Green.

Paint shoe Copper. Paint buttons on shoe Black.

Paint wing with 2 coats of Glittering Gold.

Paint star in hand Ruby and Gold (see photo).

Paint remaining star Gold.

Use desired colors of paint to outline painted designs.

3 Tie ribbon in bow. Glue bow to angel's head. Let dry. Do not wash overalls for at least 1 week. Turn overalls wrong side out, wash by hand, and hang to dry.

Design by Jane Cardinal and Inga Johns/ Duncan Enterprises

Angel and Star

Ice Cream Treat

Stitch a strip of fabric around the hem of a T-shirt to make a dress. Fuse fabric cutouts to the shirt for the ice-cream cones.

Materials

T-shirt
Floral print fabric for skirt (See Step 1.)
Thread to match fabric
Fabric scraps: floral print, brown print
Aleene's Fusible Web™
Ice-cream cone cookie cutter
White paper
Cardboard covered with waxed paper
Dimensional paints: light pink, light brown
2 (12") lengths ¼"-wide ribbon
Aleene's OK to Wash-It™ Glue

Directions

Note: See page 5 for tips on working with fusible web.

1 Wash and dry shirt and fabrics; do not use fabric softener in washer or dryer. Measure around bottom of shirt. Multiply this measurement by 2½. Put shirt on child and measure from bottom of shirt to determine desired length of skirt. Add 1" to this measurement. Cut floral print fabric to these measurements for skirt.

2 Turn under ¼" twice along 1 long edge of fabric and stitch for hem. Run 2 gathering threads along remaining long edge of fabric. With right sides facing and raw edges aligned, stitch short ends of fabric together to form tube. Pull threads to gather skirt to fit bottom of shirt. With right sides facing and gathered edge aligned with hemmed edge of shirt, stitch skirt to shirt.

3 Fuse web to wrong side of floral print scraps and brown print scraps. Trace cookie cutter on white paper to make patterns for ice-cream scoop and cone. Cut out patterns. Transfer patterns to fabric scraps and cut 3 scoops from floral print and 3 cones from brown print. Fuse scoops and cones to dress.

4 Place cardboard covered with waxed paper inside dress. Outline scoop with light pink paint. Let dry. Outline cone and add details with light brown paint. Let dry.

5 Tie each ribbon length in bow. Glue 1 bow to each sleeve of dress. Let dry.

6 Do not wash dress for at least 1 week. Turn dress wrong side out, wash by hand, and hang to dry.

Design by Heidi Borchers, SCD/Aleene's

Watercolor Magic

Use non-aerosol spray paints to create the watercolor effects shown on these shirts.

Materials

3 white T-shirts
Waxed paper
Delta Color Mist™: Purple Iris, Victorian Teal, Navy Blue, Sunflower Yellow
Spray bottle filled with clean water
Star stencils
Lace

Directions

For each, lay shirt right side up on work surface covered with waxed paper.

For watercolor-effect shirt, spray shirt lightly with Purple Iris and Navy Blue, placing colors on shirt as desired. Spray shirt with water to blend colors. Spray shirt with Victorian Teal and Sunflower Yellow, placing colors on shirt as desired. Spray shirt with water to blend colors. Let dry. In same manner, paint back of shirt.

For shirt with stars, tape stencil in place on shirt. Cover areas of shirt that will remain unpainted with waxed paper. Spray uncovered areas of shirt with 1 or more colors of Color Mist. Let dry. Remove stencils and waxed paper to spray unpainted areas of shirt with contrasting colors. Let dry. In same manner, paint back of shirt.

For shirt with lace design, tape lace in place on shirt. Spray shirt with desired colors of Color Mist. Let dry. Remove lace. In same manner, paint back of shirt.

Designs by Joyce Bennett, SCD, CCD, CPD/Delta Technical Coatings

DUDS TO DYE FOR

Tie-dye a shirt and a pair of socks with a rainbow of colors.

Materials
Rainbow Rock Tie-Dye Kit
White cotton T-shirt
Thread or dental floss (optional)
Rubber bands
Rubber gloves
Plastic dishpan
Plastic wrap
Tall kitchen plastic bag
1 pair white socks

Directions for shirt

Note: Be sure to read directions from Tie-Dye kit before beginning project.

1 With right side out, fold shirt in half lengthwise. Lightly sketch half heart on 1 side of shirt.

2 To gather shirt with stitching, run gathering thread along sketched line, using thread or dental floss. Pull to gather shirt. Bind gathered shirt tightly with rubber bands, placing first rubber band on stitched line. Place 2 or 3 more rubber bands on shirt at intervals of about 2".

To gather shirt without stitching, dip shirt into water to saturate and wring out excess water. With sketched line up, lay folded shirt flat on work surface covered with plastic wrap. Finger-pleat shirt along sketched line. Bind pleated shirt tightly with rubber bands, placing first rubber band on sketched line. Place 2 or 3 more rubber bands on shirt at intervals of about 2".

3 Put on rubber gloves. Referring to kit directions, fill dishpan with water and stir in soda ash. Place shirt into mixture and let soak for 20 minutes.

4 Cover work surface with plastic wrap. Layer folded paper towels on plastic wrap to catch excess dye. Remove shirt from soda ash bath, squeeze out excess water, and place shirt on prepared surface. Add water to dye bottles according to kit directions and shake to mix.

5 Cover unbound area of shirt with plastic bag to keep it free from dye. Squirt dye on bound area of shirt, beginning at tip with turquoise. In same manner, squirt bound area of shirt with fuchsia and then yellow dyes, overlapping colors as desired. Be sure to saturate all bound areas of shirt with dye to get rainbow effect. Be sure dye gets into folds of bound areas of shirt.

6 To dye remainder of shirt, remove plastic bag. Add water to bottle of turquoise dye as needed. Apply turquoise dye to all undyed areas of shirt, adding water to dye bottle as needed.

7 Wrap shirt with plastic wrap and let set 8 hours. Fill dishpan with clean water and rinse shirt thoroughly. Remove rubber bands and gathering thread. Dispose of dirty water. Fill dishpan with clean water and rinse shirt again. Repeat until shirt rinses clean. Wash and dry shirt, using washing machine and dryer.

Directions for socks

Note: Be sure to read directions from Tie-Dye kit before beginning project.

Place socks together with edges aligned. Bind socks tightly with rubber bands, placing rubber bands as desired. Refer to steps 3 and 4 of shirt to soak socks in soda ash mixture and to prepare work surface. Squirt socks with dye as desired. Repeat Step 7 as for shirt to set dye.

Designs by Sulfiati Harris

Snowman Cardigan

Braid strips of fabric and then coil the braids to form the circles for the snowman.

Materials

1 dark green Jerzee's sweatshirt
1 package dark green bias tape
Yarn darner needle (Dritz 14/18)
Pearl cotton thread: black, beige
1/8 yard red-green-and-white plaid fabric
1/4 yard each 3 different white-and-beige print fabrics
Aleene's OK to Wash-It™ Glue
1/4 yard red-and-white print fabric
Stuffing
2 buttons
Gold felt scrap
White dimensional paint

Directions

1 Wash and dry sweatshirt and fabrics; do not use fabric softener in washer or dryer. To find center front of shirt, fold shirt in half lengthwise, aligning shoulders and side seams. Press along fold. Unfold shirt. Cut along fold line. Bind cut edges of shirt with bias tape.

2 Tear 2 (1/2" x 45") strips of plaid fabric. Referring to photo, whipstitch plaid fabric along each edge at front of cardigan, using yarn darner needle. Tear 5 (1/2" x 45") strips from each white-and-beige print fabric. Braid 1 of each print fabric to form snowman's body. To make snowman, coil braids to form 1 (3½"-diameter) circle for head, 1 (4" x 5½") oval for center, and 1 (5¼" x 6") oval for bottom. Referring to photo, glue circle and ovals in place on cardigan front. Let dry.

3 Transfer pattern to red-and-white print fabric and cut 2 hats. Tear 1 (2½" x 45") strip for scarf from remaining red-and-white print fabric. With wrong sides facing and raw edges aligned, whipstitch hat pieces together, using black pearl cotton thread. Stuff hat lightly before stitching is complete. Glue hat in place on cardigan. Let dry. Fold 2½" x 45" strip in half widthwise. Knot strip 4½" from folded end. Glue scarf in place on snowman. Let dry.

4 Stitch buttons in place on snowman for eyes, using beige pearl cotton thread. Cut triangle for nose from felt scrap (see photo). Glue nose in place on snowman. Let dry. Referring to photo, write "Let it snow!" on cardigan, using dimensional paint. Let dry. Tear 1/2"-wide strips from remaining white-and-beige fabrics. For snowflakes, stitch French knots on cardigan with 1/2"-wide fabric strips.

5 Tear 1" x 6" strips from all remaining fabrics. Knot center of each strip. Glue knots evenly spaced around neckline of cardigan (see photo). Let dry. Do not wash cardigan for at least 1 week. Turn cardigan wrong side out, wash by hand, and hang to dry.

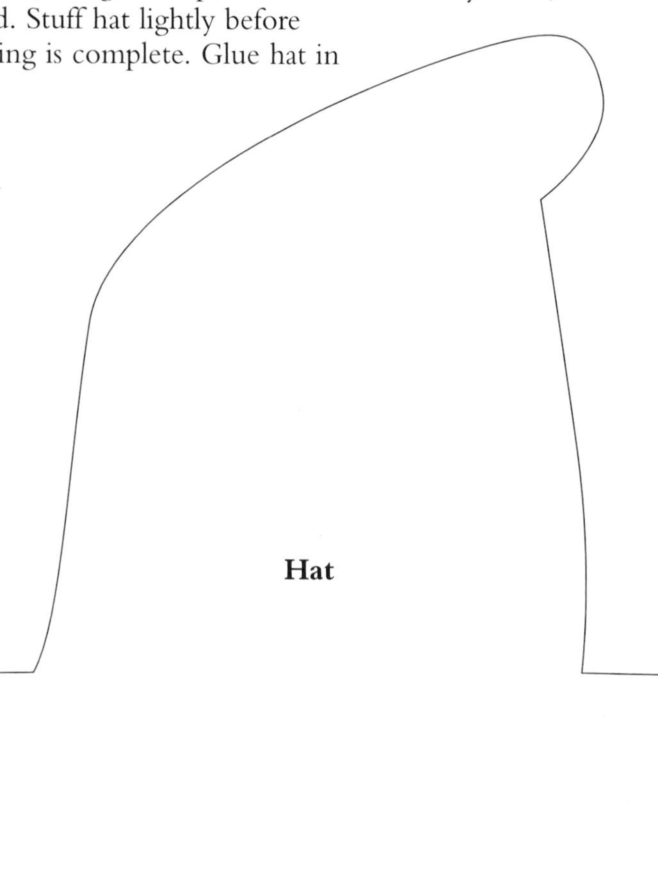

Design by Rebecca Hermann/Jo-Ann Fabrics and Crafts

Let it snow!

Spring Garden Vest

Sponge-painted flowers make this vest a blooming wonder.

Materials

Vest
Natural sea sponges
1"-wide lightweight cardboard strips: ½" long, ¾" long, 1" long, 3" long
Pop-up craft sponges
Aleene's Enhancers™ Textile Medium
Aleene's Premium-Coat™ Acrylic Paints: True Yellow, Medium Green, True Green, True Lavender, True Violet, True Fuchsia

Directions

1 Wash and dry vest; do not use fabric softener in washer or dryer. For grass, apply tape horizontally across vest at desired height from bottom of vest. For each color of acrylic paint, mix equal parts textile medium and paint. Dip dampened natural sea sponges into desired colors of acrylic paint to paint grass (see photo). Let dry. Remove tape. For vertical lines of grass, dip edge of 1" long piece of cardboard into True Green paint and press on vest.

2 Transfer patterns to pop-up sponges and cut 1 star flower and 1 leaf. Also cut 1 (2"-diameter) circle for round flowers and 1 (1"-diameter) circle for flower centers from pop-up sponges. Dip each sponge into water to expand and wring out excess water. Dip sponge into desired color of paint and blot excess paint on paper towel. Press sponge onto vest as desired. Repeat to paint designs on vest as desired (see photo). Wash sponge thoroughly before dipping into different paint color. Let dry.

3 For flower stems, dip edge of 3" piece of cardboard into True Green paint and press on vest. In same manner, paint lines on round flowers, grid on center of star flowers, and lines on leaves, using assorted cardboard pieces. In same manner, paint accent lines randomly on vest (see photo), using cardboard pieces. Let dry.

4 Do not wash vest for at least 1 week. Turn vest wrong side out, wash by hand, and hang to dry.

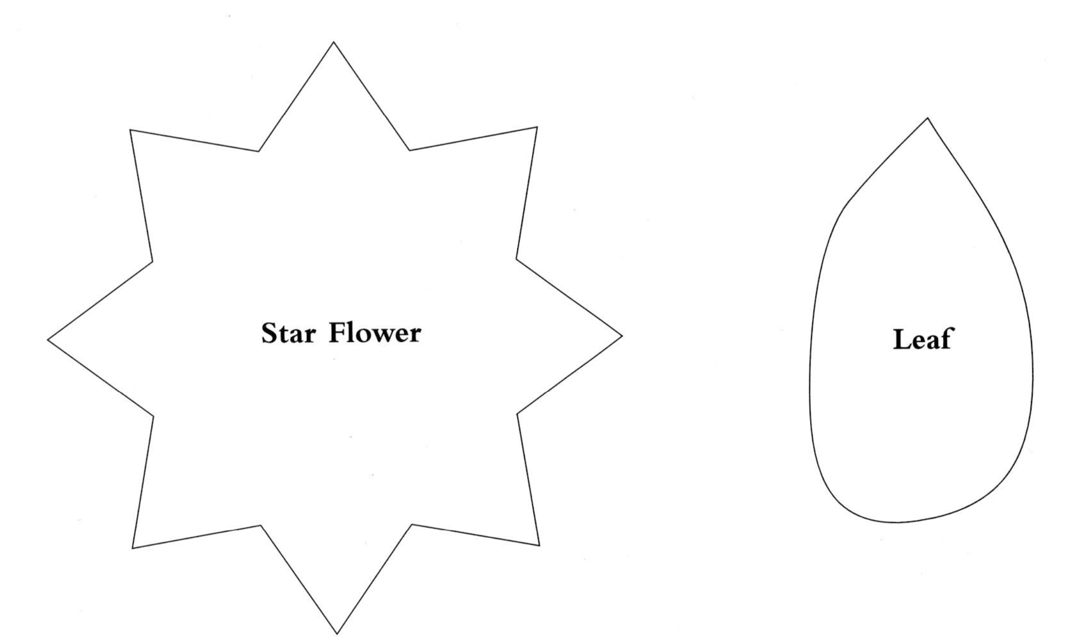

Design by Chris Wallace/Duncan Enterprises

Super Dad Apron & Hat

Apply felt letters and fabric stars to an apron and hat for a stellar gift for Dad.

Materials

White apron
White chef's hat
Red-white-and-blue star print fabric
Aleene's Fusible Web™
Blue Rainbow Presto Felt Letters: 2 As, 4 Ds, 1 E, 1 P, 1 R, 1 S, 1 U (See note.)
Aleene's OK to Wash-It™ Glue
Star rhinestones: red, white, blue
Aleene's Jewel-It™ Glue

Directions

Note: If desired, use alphabet stencils to cut letters from blue felt. Glue letters to apron as described in Step 1.

See page 5 for tips on working with fusible web.

1 Wash and dry apron, hat, and fabric; do not use fabric softener in washer or dryer. Fuse web to wrong side fabric. Transfer pattern to fabric and cut 9 stars. Referring to photo, fuse stars to apron and hat. Remove paper backing from each felt letter. Glue letters to apron and hat, using OK to Wash-It Glue. Let dry.

2 To glue each star rhinestone to apron and hat, squeeze small puddle of Jewel-It Glue on item in desired position. Press 1 star rhinestone into glue so that glue comes up around sides of jewel. Let dry.

3 Do not wash apron or hat for at least 1 week. Wash by hand and hang to dry.

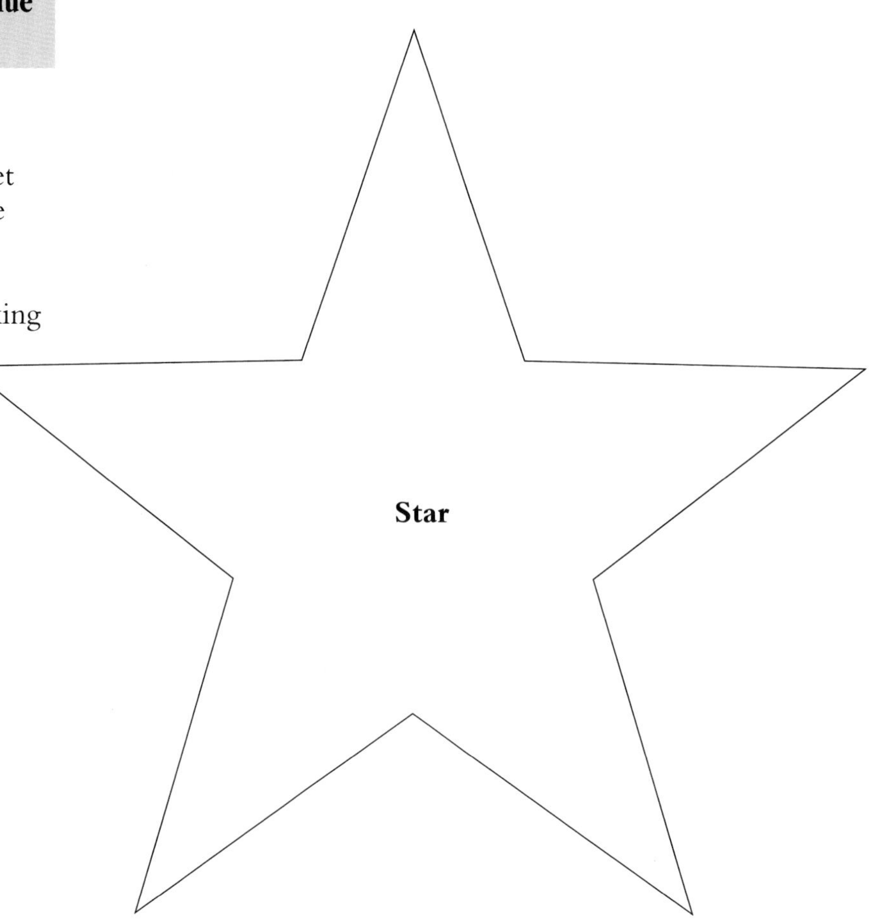

Designs by Janna Britton/Aleene's

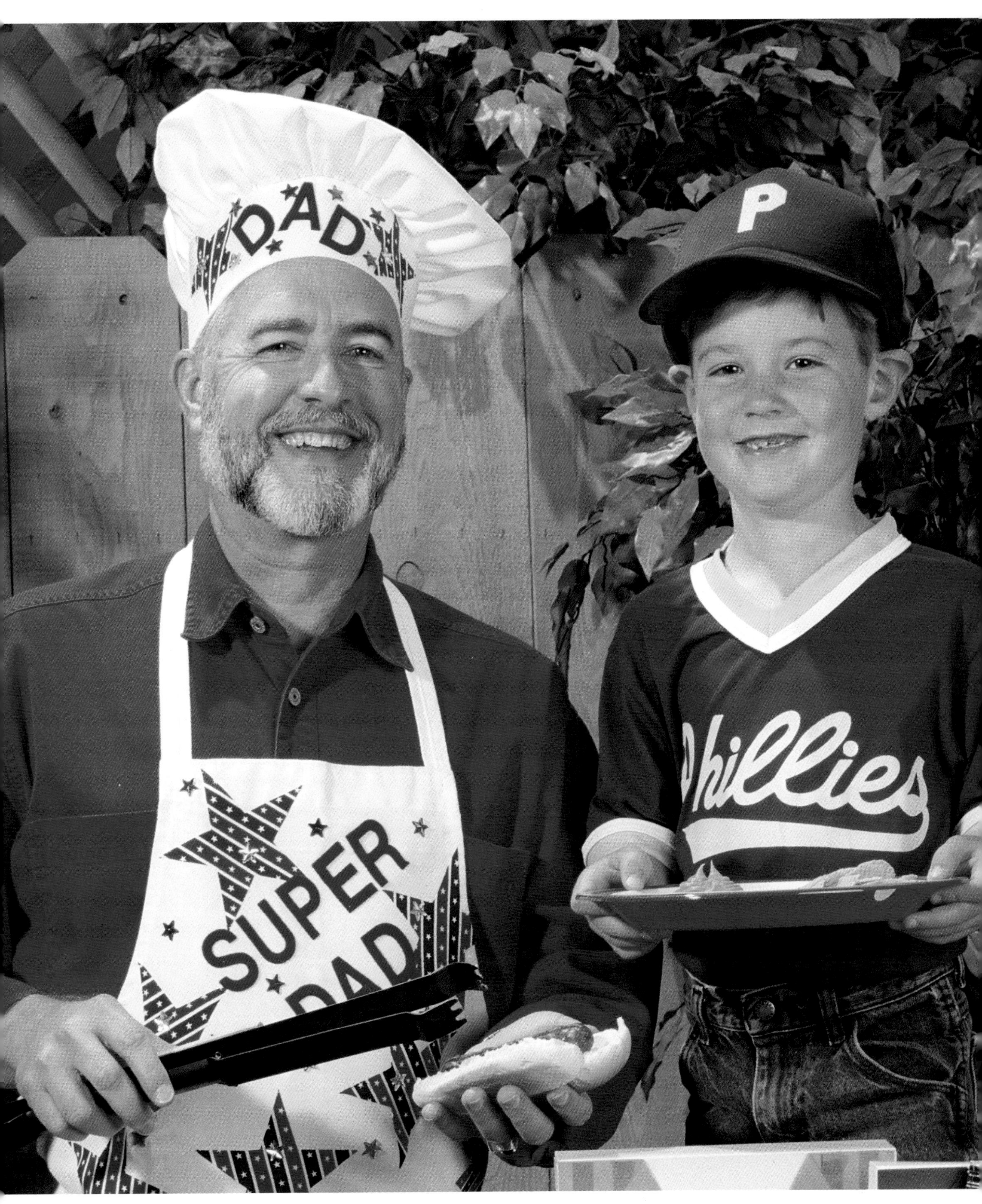
DAD
SUPER
P

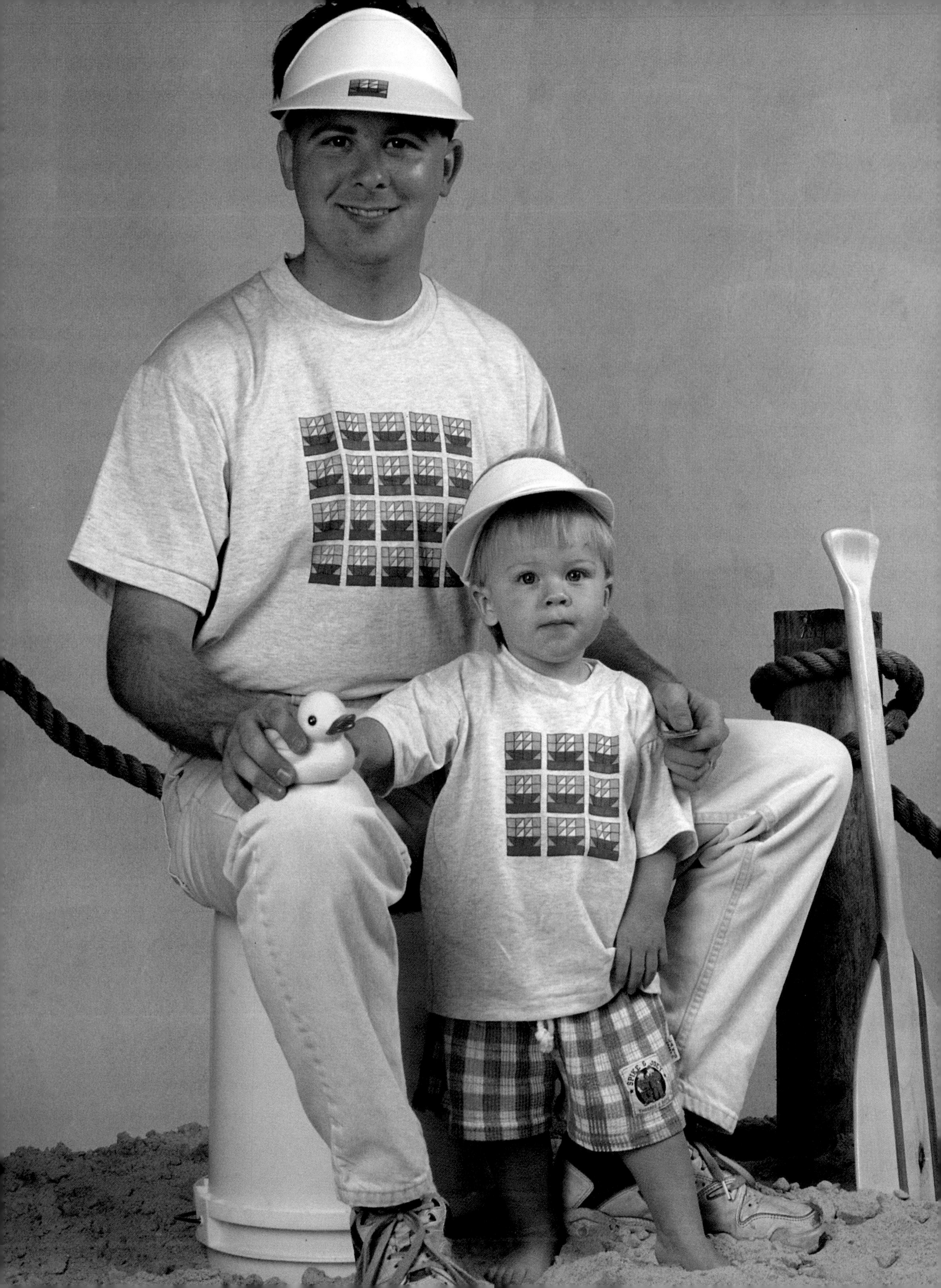

Ahoy, Mate

Stamp quilt-block sailboats on wearables to make matching T-shirts for father and son.

Materials

- Pelle's Fabric Ink & Pad Set
- Small spatula
- Pelle's See-Thru Stamp: Sailboat Block (#216)
- Scrap of muslin
- T-shirts in desired sizes
- Fabric visor
- Unscented baby wipes
- Cardboard covered with waxed paper
- Y & C Fabricmate Brush-Tip Markers: Red (#1200B), Cobalt Blue (#120AC), Sky Blue (#120FS)
- Teflon pressing cloth

Directions

Note: To order Pelle's Fabric Ink & Pad Set and Sailboat Block See-Thru Stamp, call or write Pele Fleming, P.O. Box 242, Davenport, CA 95017; (408) 425-4743.

Be sure to read directions from fabric ink and pad set before beginning project.

1 Slowly ink blank foam pad, using small spatula. Apply ink until pad is squishy. Ink should be absorbed by pad, not puddling on top of pad. To ink stamp, tap stamp lightly up and down on pad; do not press stamp into pad. Practice stamping on scrap of muslin before stamping on project. Place muslin or project on smooth, firm surface for best results. Press stamp on printing surface, being sure all areas of stamp come into contact with surface. Do not rock stamp on surface. Re-ink stamp after each printing. Clean stamp as needed, using baby wipes.

2 **For each,** wash and dry shirt; do not use fabric softener in washer or dryer.

For large shirt, center first sailboat on shirt front about 4½" below neckline. Referring to photo, stamp additional sailboats on shirt front, leaving about ⅛" between each.

For small shirt, center first sailboat on shirt front about 2½" below neckline. Referring to photo, stamp additional sailboats on shirt front, leaving about ⅛" between each.

For visor, center and stamp 1 sailboat on bill of visor.

3 **For each,** place cardboard covered with waxed paper inside shirt. Working with 1 color at a time, color stamped sailboats as desired, using markers. Let marker ink dry for 24 hours. To heat-set colors, place Teflon pressing cloth over design. Press Teflon cloth with hot, dry iron.

Designs by Pele D. Fleming

Strawberry Fields FOREVER

Purchase ready-made prairie points and yo-yos to make the strawberries on this sweatshirt jacket.

Materials

Dark green sweatshirt
Aleene's OK to Wash-It™ Glue
2 strips red-and-white Prairie Points from Shafaii (#0392-58)
4 large red dot Prairie Points from Shafaii (#0393-17)
8 medium green dot fabric Yo-yos from Shafaii (#0346-05)
Thread: red, green
10 small white fabric Yo-yos from Shafaii (#0345-11)
Dimensional paints: pearl green, yellow

Directions

1 Wash and dry sweatshirt; do not use fabric softener in washer or dryer. To find center front of shirt, fold shirt in half lengthwise, aligning shoulders and side seams. Press along fold. Unfold shirt. Cut along fold line. Turn under ½" along each cut edge of sweatshirt and glue for hem. Let dry. Align stitched edge of strip of Prairie Points with hemmed edge of sweatshirt and glue 1 strip to each front edge of jacket so that Prairie Points extend beyond edge of jacket. Let dry.

2 For each strawberry, run gathering thread along stitched edge of each red dot Prairie Point. Pull to gather Prairie Point into heart shape and secure thread. To add 2 leaves to each strawberry, fold 2 green yo-yos in half, sandwiching top of strawberry between each (see photo). Stitch leaves to strawberry. Referring to photo, glue strawberries and white yo-yos for flowers to jacket. Let dry. Draw vines, tendrils, stems on strawberries, and additional leaves on jacket with pearl green paint (see photo). Center and paint 3 yellow dots on each white yo-yo for flower center. Let dry.

3 Do not wash jacket for at least 1 week. Turn jacket wrong side out, wash by hand in cold water, and lay flat to dry.

Gather the stitched edge of purchased prairie points to make strawberries to adorn a green sweatshirt jacket.

Design by Debby Newman/Shafaii

Holiday

Deck your halls for the holidays with these festive designs.

Page 122

Page 134

Page 140

Page 114

Page 133

Crafting

Tidings of Joy

Hang this heavenly mobile in a large window for a dazzling display.

Materials

Aleene's Clear Shrink-It™ Plastic
Aleene's 3-D Foiling Glue™
Aleene's Gold Crafting Foil™
Glitter (optional)
Assorted colors tissue paper or 1-ply sheer paper napkins
Fabric softener dryer sheets
Aleene's Reverse Collage Glue™
Paintbrush
Hole punch
Monofilament
Plastic crystal drops

Directions

1 Lay 1 piece of Shrink-It over angel pattern (on page 108). Trace all pattern lines onto Shrink-It, using 3-D Foiling Glue. Let dry. (Glue will be opaque and sticky when dry. Glue must be thoroughly dry before foil is applied.) To apply gold foil, lay foil dull side down on top of glue lines. Using finger, gently but firmly press foil onto glue, completely covering glue lines with foil. Peel away foil paper. If any part of glue is not covered, reapply foil as needed.

2 For angel, cut pieces of tissue paper or paper napkins slightly larger than design areas (see photo). For wings, cut pieces of dryer sheets slightly larger than design areas. Lay Shrink-It, foil side down, on work surface. Working over 1 design area at a time, brush coat of Reverse Collage Glue on Shrink-It in desired position. If desired, sprinkle glitter onto wet glue. Press paper piece into glue-covered area. Working from outside edges to center, use fingers or brush to gently wrinkle paper, shaping it to fit design area. Brush coat of Reverse Collage Glue on top of paper. In same manner, apply paper pieces and dryer sheet pieces to remainder of design. With edges aligned, press another piece of Shrink-It onto design while glue is still wet. Let dry. Cut out angel.

In same manner, make 6 large stars and 10 small stars.

3 Punch holes in angel where indicated on pattern. Punch 1 hole in each star. Referring to photo, hang stars and crystal drops from bottom of angel, using monofilament. Add monofilament hanger to top of angel.

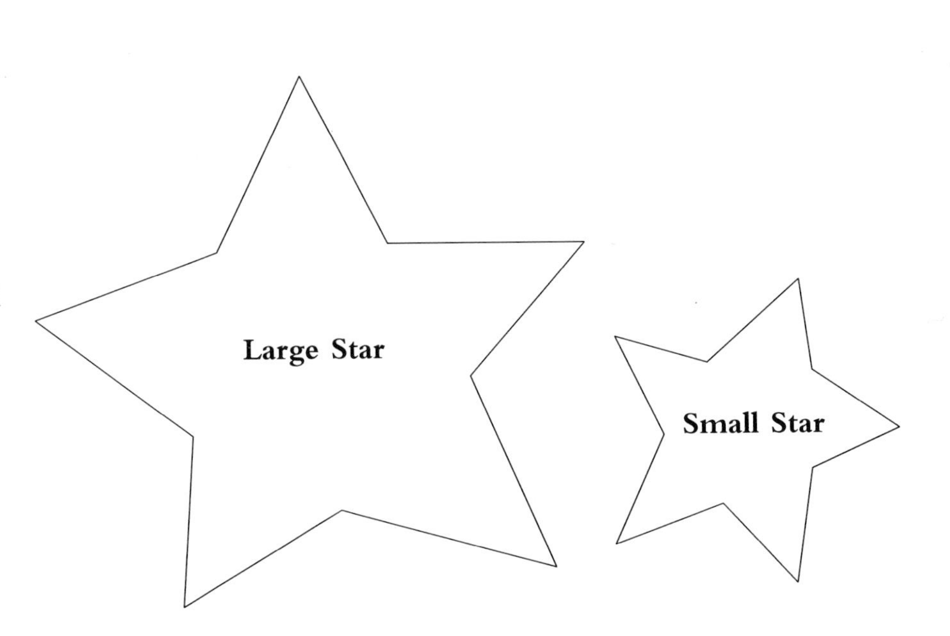

Design by Darsee Lett and Pattie Donham/Hobby Lobby Stores

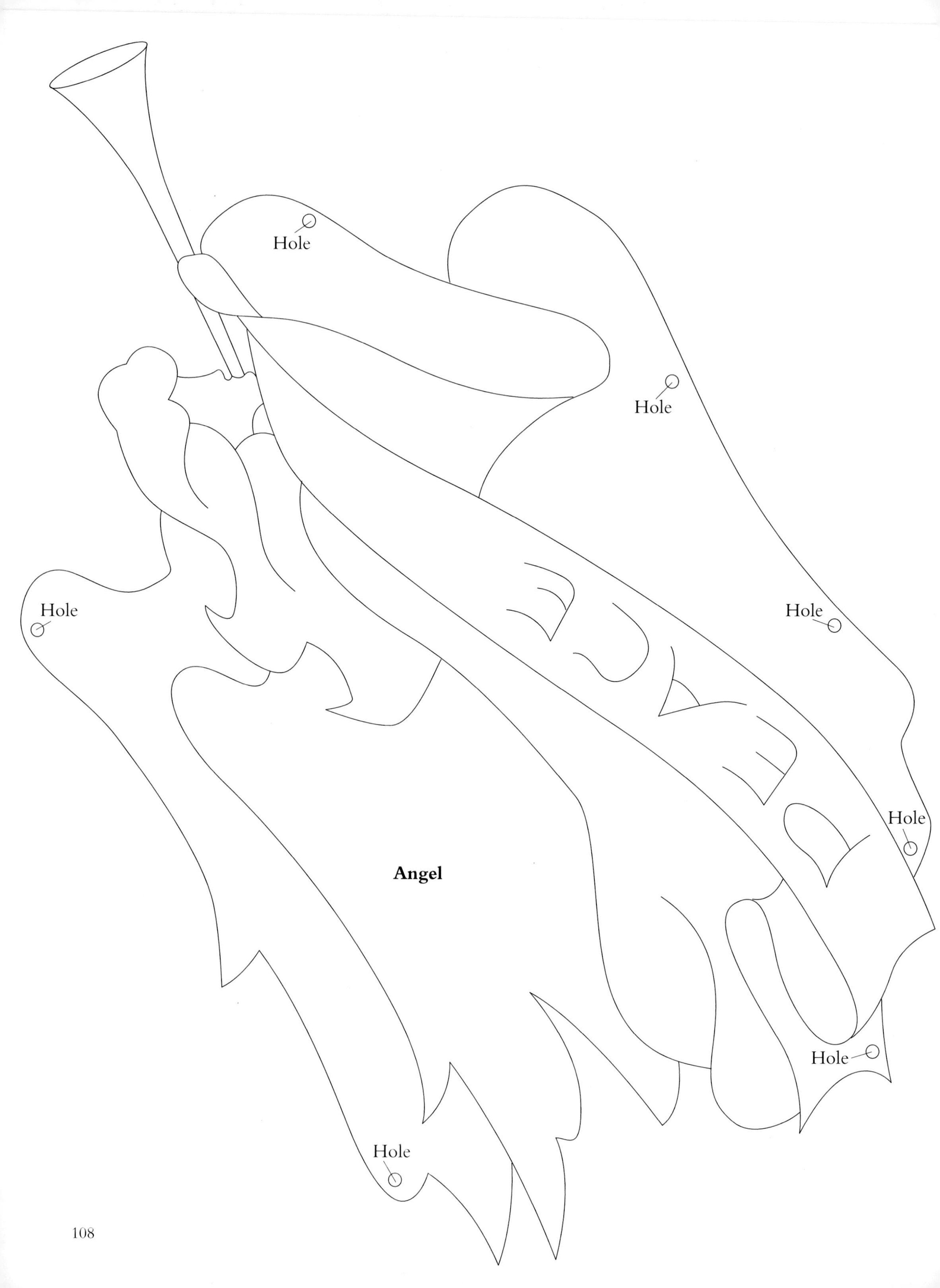
Hole
Hole
Hole
Hole
Hole
Angel
Hole
Hole

Design by Jo-Ann Fabrics and Crafts

Touch of Gold

Add lots of golden trims to an artificial wreath for an extravagant holiday decoration.

Materials

Design Master spray paints: Hunter Green, Shimmer Gold, Brilliant Gold, Glossy Wood Tone, Glitter Opal Essence
24"-diameter artificial evergreen wreath
8 white plastic snowflakes
16 white plastic twigs
Newspaper or waxed paper
8 pinecones
80 small gold ball ornaments
Aleene's Designer Tacky Glue™ and hot-glue gun and glue sticks (See note.)
26-gauge florist's wire
4 yards gold metallic cording

Directions

Note: To use Designer Tacky Glue in combination with glue gun, apply small amounts of each glue for strong and permanent bond.

1 Following manufacturer's directions, spray-paint wreath Hunter Green. Let dry. Highlight wreath with Shimmer Gold. Let dry. Lay snowflakes and twigs on work surface covered with newspaper or waxed paper. Spray-paint snowflakes and twigs Brilliant Gold. Let dry. Lightly spray-paint snowflakes with Wood Tone. Let dry. Spray-paint pinecones Wood Tone. Let dry. Highlight pinecones with Shimmer Gold. Let dry. Lightly spray-paint ornaments with Opal Essence. Let dry.

2 Fluff and shape wreath as desired. Glue snowflakes, twigs, and pinecones in place on wreath. Let dry. Attach clusters of ornaments to wreath, using florist's wire. Loop cording around wreath as desired.

Ping-Pong Christmas

Craft these easy ornaments to adorn your tree, embellish packages, or sell at a holiday bazaar.

Materials

For each: **2 Ping-Pong balls**
Drill with 1/16" bit
Toothpick
Aleene's Designer Tacky Glue™

For snowman: **Black construction paper**
6" length silver metallic thread
2 (3/8"-diameter) light brown pom-poms
Print fabric scrap
Pinking shears
Aleene's Premium-Coat™ Acrylic Paints: Black, True Red
Fine-tip paintbrush
Dimensional paints: black, orange

For Santa: **Red spray paint**
Felt scraps: white, red
6" length gold metallic thread
Pom-poms: 1 (1/2"-diameter) white, 1 (1/4"-diameter) red
Black dimensional paint

Directions

1 **For Santa,** spray-paint 1 ball red. Let dry. **For each,** drill 1 hole in each ball. Dip 1 end of toothpick into glue and push into hole in 1 ball. Dip free end of toothpick into glue and push into hole in remaining ball. Push balls together and glue to form body. Let dry.

2 **For snowman,** cut 1 (1" x 2") strip for hat crown, 1 (2"-diameter) circle for hat brim, and 1 (1 1/4"-diameter) circle for hat top from black paper. Center and poke 1 small hole in hat top. Roll hat crown to form tube. Overlap ends and glue. Let dry. Center and glue hat crown on hat brim. Let dry. Fold metallic thread in half to form loop and knot ends. Thread fold of thread through hole in hat top. Glue knot to hat top. Glue hat top to hat crown. Let dry. Glue hat to snowman's head. Glue 1 pom-pom to each side of head for ear muffs. Let dry. For scarf, cut 1 (1/4" x 3") strip of fabric, using pinking shears. Wrap and glue scarf around snowman's neck. Let dry. Paint mouth Black and cheeks True Red, using paintbrush. Let dry. Paint eyes and buttons with black dimensional paint. Paint nose with orange dimensional paint. Let dry.

For Santa, transfer patterns to felt and cut 1 beard and 1 mustache from white, and 1 hat from red. From remaining white felt, cut 1 (1/4" x 1") strip for collar and 1 (1/4" x 5") strip for hat trim. Glue collar in place on Santa's body. Let dry. Fold metallic thread in half to form loop and knot ends. Curve hat into cone shape, overlapping straight edges and catching knot of hanger in hat tip, and glue. Let dry. Referring to photo, glue beard, mustache, and hat in place on Santa's head. Glue remaining white felt strip around bottom of hat for trim. Let dry. Glue white pom-pom to hat tip. Glue red pom-pom nose to face. Let dry. Paint eyes with black dimensional paint. Let dry.

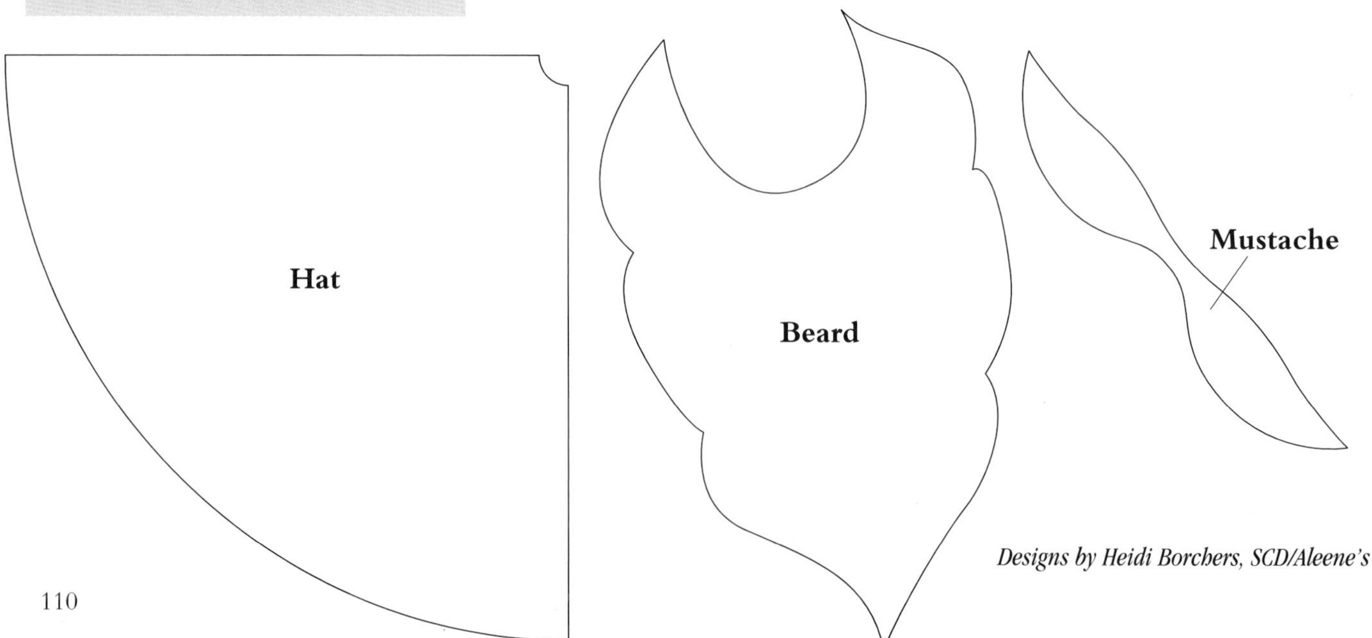

Designs by Heidi Borchers, SCD/Aleene's

EASY FABRIC Garlands

Trace a pattern onto fused layers of fabric. Fold the fabric accordion style and then cut out a holiday shape to make a garland.

Materials

For each: **Aleene's Fusible Web™**
12" x 34" strip fabric
Aleene's Opake Shrink-It™ Plastic
Awl or ice pick
1 yard 1/16"-wide picot ribbon

Directions for 1 garland

Fuse web to cover wrong side of fabric strip. With web sides facing, fold fabric strip in half lengthwise and fuse. Transfer desired pattern to Shrink-It and cut out. Using desired pattern as guide, accordion-fold fabric strip to match width of template and press. Unfold fabric. With fold lines of template aligned with fold line of fabric, trace pattern onto fabric. Carefully cut out shape, but *do not cut along fold lines.* Flip template onto next section of fabric, aligning fold lines as before, and trace. In same manner, trace and cut out shapes to complete garland. Poke 1 hole at each end of garland, using awl. Cut ribbon in half. Thread 1 ribbon length through each hole and tie in bow.

Designs by Hancock Fabrics

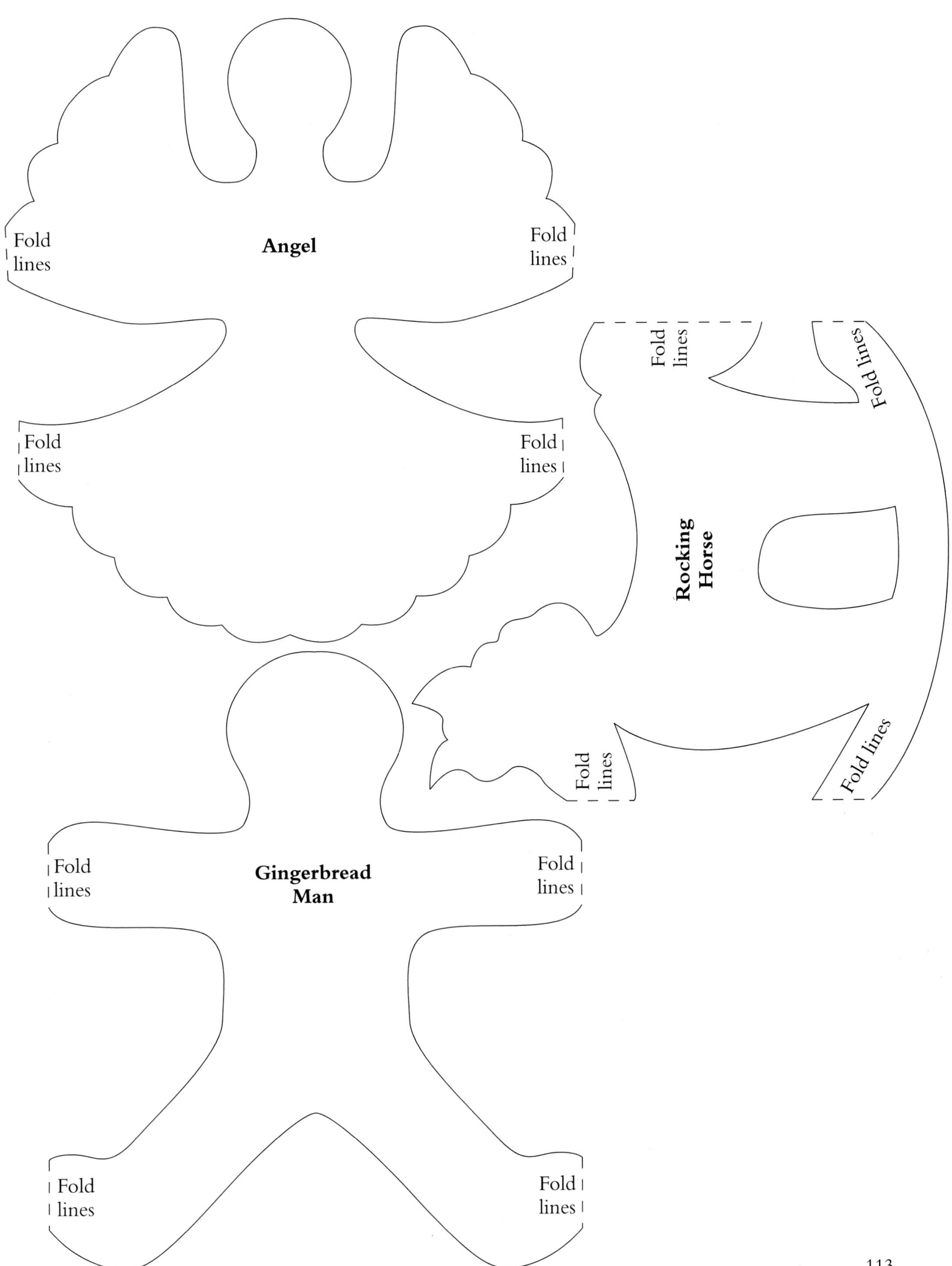
Fold lines
Angel
Fold lines
Fold lines
Fold lines
Fold lines
Fold lines
Rocking Horse
Fold lines
Fold lines
Fold lines
Fold lines
Gingerbread Man
Fold lines
Fold lines
Fold lines

Dear Santa,
Gone South
for the
winter
Happy
Holidays
Birdie

FOR THE Birds

Decorate wooden birdhouses to make a set of ornaments for your tree or for a table or mantel arrangement.

Materials

Delta Color Mist™: Christmas Red, Hunter Green
1 Walnut Hollow birdhouse
3 miniature birdhouses
Spanish moss
Pinecones
Delta Highlighter Mist™: Pale Gold Highlighter
Aleene's Tacky Glue™
Delta Fantasy Snow™
Wooden craft stick
4 yards 2½"-wide printed bark paper ribbon
24-gauge florist's wire
3 yards gold cording
Gold holly leaves
Beige paper scrap
Fine-tip permanent marker
Artificial greenery
Assorted trims
Delta Glitter Mist™: Gold Glitter

Directions

1 For each birdhouse, spray-paint birdhouse Christmas Red, moss Hunter Green, and pinecones Pale Gold. Let dry. Glue moss to roof and base of each birdhouse. Let dry. Apply Fantasy Snow to roof, base, and perch of each birdhouse, using craft stick. Let dry.

2 For large birdhouse, cut or tear 4 lengthwise strips from paper ribbon. Handling 2 strips of ribbon as 1, make multilooped bow. Secure bow with florist's wire. Set remaining 2 strips aside for another use. Center and glue bow on roof of birdhouse. Let dry. Cut gold cording into 3 (1-yard) lengths. Make multilooped bow with each of 2 (1-yard) lengths, securing each bow with florist's wire. Glue 1 gold bow on each side of paper ribbon bow. Let dry. Glue pinecones and gold holly leaves to roof as desired. Let dry.

3 For each sign, trim paper scrap to desired size. Write desired message on paper with marker. Wrap ends of paper around pen to curl. Glue sign to birdhouse. Let dry.

4 For each miniature birdhouse, cut 3 (4") lengths and 3 (8") lengths from remaining yard of gold cording. Fold each 4" length in half to make loop and knot ends. To add 1 hanger to each birdhouse, center and glue 1 knot on roof of birdhouse. Tie each 8" length in bow. Glue 1 bow to roof of each birdhouse. Referring to photo, glue pinecones, artificial greenery, and assorted trims to each birdhouse as desired. Let dry.

5 For each birdhouse, spray-paint birdhouse with Gold Glitter as desired.

Designs by Joyce Bennett, SCD, CCD, CPD/Delta Technical Coatings

A CHORUS OF *Angels*

Use gold mesh ribbon to make a trio of elegant angels for a heavenly centerpiece.

Materials

For each: **9"-high Styrofoam cone**
Gold spray paint
3"-wide gold mesh ribbon: 5 (20") lengths, 1 (17") length
Gold straight pins
12" length 3/8"-wide gold metallic flat braid
12" length gold metallic chenille stem
Gold wired cording: 2 (1") lengths, 3 (5") lengths
7/16"-wide gold wire-edged ribbon: 1 (15") length, 1 (3") length
Aleene's Designer Tacky Glue™
1½ yards 5/8"-wide gold wire-edged ribbon
2"-diameter Styrofoam ball
1 yard 2⅝"-wide gold mesh wire-edged ribbon
Florist's wire
10" length gold garland or gold miniature musical instrument (optional)

Directions for 1 angel

1 Spray-paint cone. Let dry. Pin 1 (20") ribbon length over top of cone, pinning along ribbon edges to base of cone. In same manner, pin second 20" ribbon length at right angles to first ribbon to completely cover cone, shaping ribbon at top of cone for shoulders. Trim ribbon ends even with bottom of cone. Wrap and glue 3/8"-wide braid around bottom of cone. Let dry.

2 For arms, roll 17" length of gold mesh ribbon around chenille stem, tucking ends inside. Wrap 1 (1") length of cording around arm about ½" from each end to form hands. Pin center of arms to top of cone. Shape arms as desired. Pin center of each remaining 20" ribbon length to top of cone for skirt (see photo). Trim ribbon ends to desired length. Notch ribbon ends. Wrap 15" length of wire-edged ribbon around cone to form waist. Twist ribbon ends to secure. Scrunch ribbon and let ends ravel.

3 For head, wrap 5/8"-wide ribbon around ball to cover, pinning ends to secure. Glue head to top of cone. Let dry. For wings, tie 2⅝"-wide ribbon in 4-loop bow without streamers; secure bow with florist's wire. Wrap 3" length of wire-edged ribbon around center of bow to cover florist's wire. Glue wings to back of angel. Let dry. Braid 5" lengths of cording. For halo, curve braided cording into circle, twisting ends together to secure. Glue halo to angel's head. Let dry. If desired, attach garland or instrument to angel's hands, using florist's wire.

Designs by Ribbon Outlet

Festive Holiday Swag

Swirl gold and maroon paints inside glass ornaments for shimmering accents on an evergreen swag.

Materials

3 iridescent glass ball ornaments
Delta Ceramcoat Gleams Paint: 14K Gold
Delta Ceramcoat Acrylic Paint: Maroon
24"-long artificial greenery swag
32" length 1½"-wide burgundy wire-edged ribbon
Aleene's Designer Tacky Glue™
3 yards 1¼"-wide gold wire-edged sheer ribbon
24-gauge florist's wire
18 gold berry picks

Directions

For each ornament, remove cap from ornament. Pour small puddle of Gold paint into ornament. Rotate ornament to coat inside of ornament with paint. Don't completely cover inside of ornament with Gold paint. Pour small puddle of Maroon paint into ornament. Rotate ornament to coat uncovered areas of ornament with paint and to mix Maroon paint with Gold paint (see photo). Pour out excess paint. Place ornament upside down on surface protected by paper towels for about 5 minutes to let remaining excess paint drain out. Let dry for 24 hours. Replace cap.

For swag, arrange burgundy ribbon on swag as desired. Glue ribbon in place as needed. Let dry. Make multilooped bow with gold ribbon and secure bow with florist's wire. Use tails of wire to attach bow to swag. Referring to photo for inspiration, glue ornaments and berry picks in place on swag. Let dry.

Design by Tracia Ledford SCD, CPD, and Katelyn Ledford/Aleene's

ARTISTIC apron

Sponge-paint a row of ornaments across the bottom of an apron and then sprinkle glitter onto the wet paint.

Materials
Pop-up craft sponges
Dimensional paints: assorted colors, gold glitter
Apron
Prisma glitter
Plaid Bow Beautiful stencil

Directions

1 Transfer patterns to sponges and cut 1 of each ornament. Dip each sponge into water to expand and wring out excess water. Dip sponge into desired color of paint and blot excess paint on paper towel. Press sponge onto apron to paint ornaments along bottom edge of apron (see photo). Sprinkle glitter onto wet paint. Let dry. Wash sponge thoroughly before dipping into different paint color.

2 Paint top on each ornament with gold glitter paint. Sprinkle glitter onto wet paint. Let dry. Outline ornament with paint to match ornament. Sprinkle glitter onto wet paint. Let dry. Embellish ornament as desired with assorted colors of paint. Sprinkle glitter onto wet paint. Let dry.

3 Stencil bow on bib of apron. Draw wavy line to "hang" each ornament from bow, using dimensional paints. Sprinkle glitter onto wet paint. Let dry. Cut close to paint lines to scallop bottom edge of apron (see photo).

Design by Joann Pearson/Michaels Stores

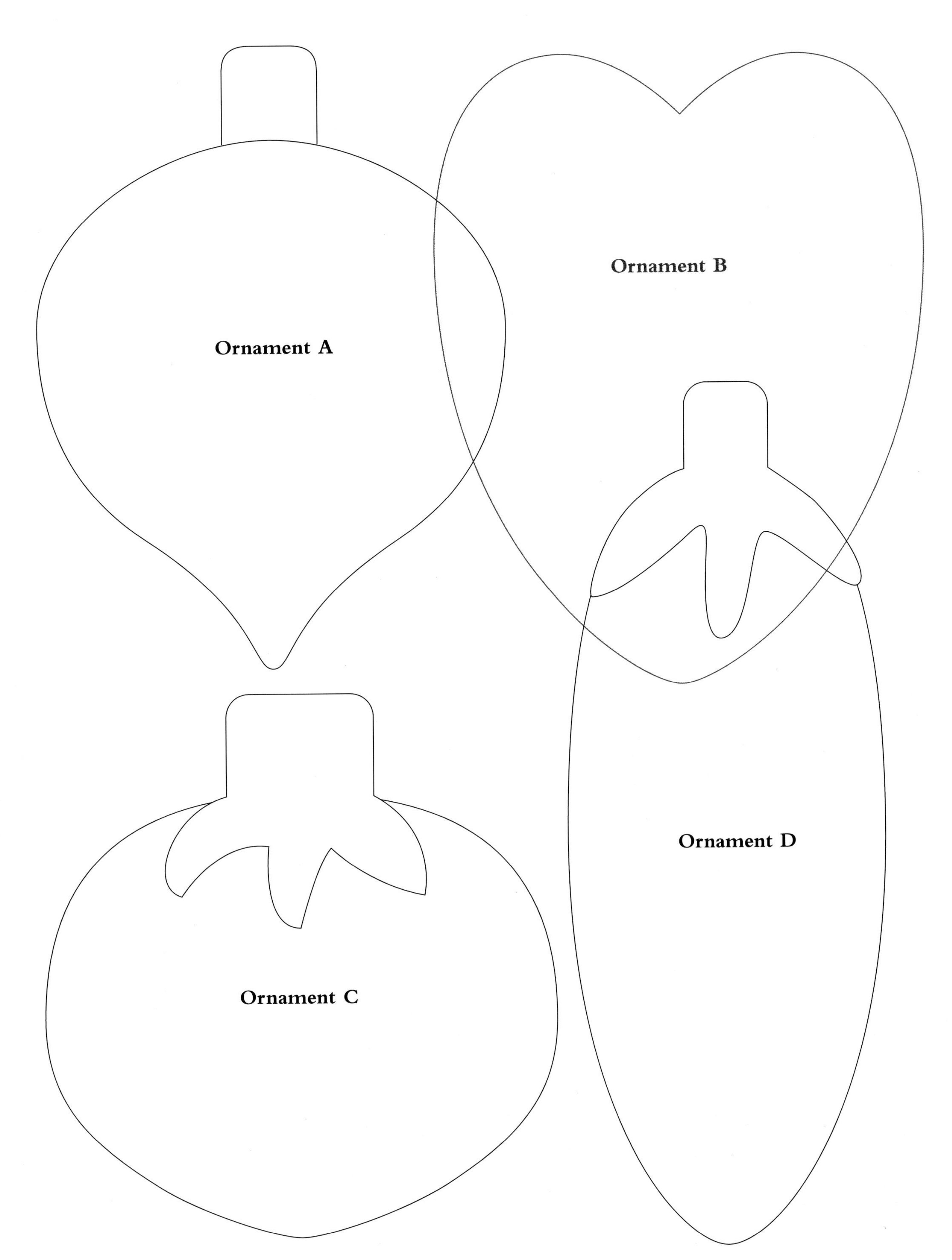
Ornament A
Ornament B
Ornament C
Ornament D

Designs by Heidi Borchers, SCD/Aleene's

Holiday Curtain Call

Spice up your curtains with a decorated grapevine wreath tieback.

Materials

For each: **7½"-diameter grapevine wreath**
1 yard 1½"-wide wire-edged ribbon
26-gauge florist's wire
5 (8") lengths gold-wrapped wire
Marker
Berry and greenery picks
White silk flowers
Aleene's Designer Tacky Glue™ and hot-glue gun and glue sticks (See note.)

Directions for 1 tieback

Note: To use Designer Tacky Glue in combination with glue gun, apply small amounts of each glue for strong and permanent bond.

Make multilooped bow with ribbon and secure bow with florist's wire. Wrap each length of gold wire around marker to coil. Referring to photo, glue coiled wire, berry and greenery picks, white silk flowers, and bow to wreath. Let dry.

Select ribbon, trims, and flowers to make a springtime or Easter tieback. Coordinate the color scheme of the tieback to match your curtain fabric.

Design by Joann Pearson/Michaels Stores

Winter WELCOME

Let this soft-sculpture snowman greet your guests next holiday season.

Materials

18"-diameter grapevine wreath
3 yards 2"-wide green checked ribbon
Aleene's Designer Tacky Glue™ and hot-glue gun and glue sticks (See note.)
Florist's wire
Quilted house ornament (optional)
14" x 24" piece cotton batting
Poly-fil® stuffing
Assorted sizes buttons: 8 black, 15 assorted colors
Christmas print fabric: 1 (2" x 12") strip, 1 (10" x 12") piece, scraps
Pinking shears
Black thread
2 small tree branches
Felt: orange, red
5" length jute

Directions

Note: To use Designer Tacky Glue in combination with glue gun, apply small amounts of each glue for strong and permanent bond.

1 Referring to photo, wrap ribbon around wreath. Cut excess ribbon. Glue ribbon ends to back of wreath. Make multilooped bow with remaining ribbon and secure bow with florist's wire. Glue bow to wreath. If desired, glue ornament to center of bow. Let dry.

2 Transfer pattern on page 126 to batting and cut 2 snowmen. Squeeze line of glue around edges of 1 snowman piece, leaving 1½" area unglued. With edges aligned, glue snowman pieces together. Let dry. Stuff snowman lightly. Glue opening closed. Let dry. Glue black buttons to snowman for eyes, mouth, and buttons on body. Let dry.

3 For scarf, trim edges of 2" x 12" fabric strip, using pinking shears. Tie scarf around snowman's neck. For hat, trim edges of 10" x 12" fabric piece, using pinking shears. Squeeze thin line of glue on right side along 1 (12") edge of fabric. Overlap 12" edges ¼" and glue to make tube. Let dry. Run gathering thread around tube about 1" from 1 end. Pull to gather tightly and secure thread. Run another gathering thread around hat about 5" from first gather. Pull to gather tightly and secure thread. Turn up open end of hat to form 1" cuff. Stuff hat lightly. Glue hat to snowman's head. Let dry.

4 Cut 2 (1") squares from fabric scraps, using pinking shears. Stitch squares to snowman, using black thread (see photo). Cut additional 1" squares and several 2" squares from remaining fabric scraps, using pinking shears. Glue squares and remaining buttons to wreath and bow as desired. Clip small holes in snowman where indicated on pattern. For arms, dip 1 end of 1 tree branch into glue. Insert end of branch through hole. Repeat for other arm. Let dry.

5 Transfer patterns on page 126 to felt and cut 1 nose from orange and 4 mittens from red. Curve nose into cone shape, overlapping straight edges, and glue. Let dry. Stuff nose lightly. Glue nose to snowman. Let dry. With edges aligned, glue 2 mitten pieces together, sandwiching 1 end of jute between straight edges. Repeat to glue remaining mitten pieces to free end of jute. Wrap center of jute around 1 arm of snowman. Glue snowman to wreath. Let dry.

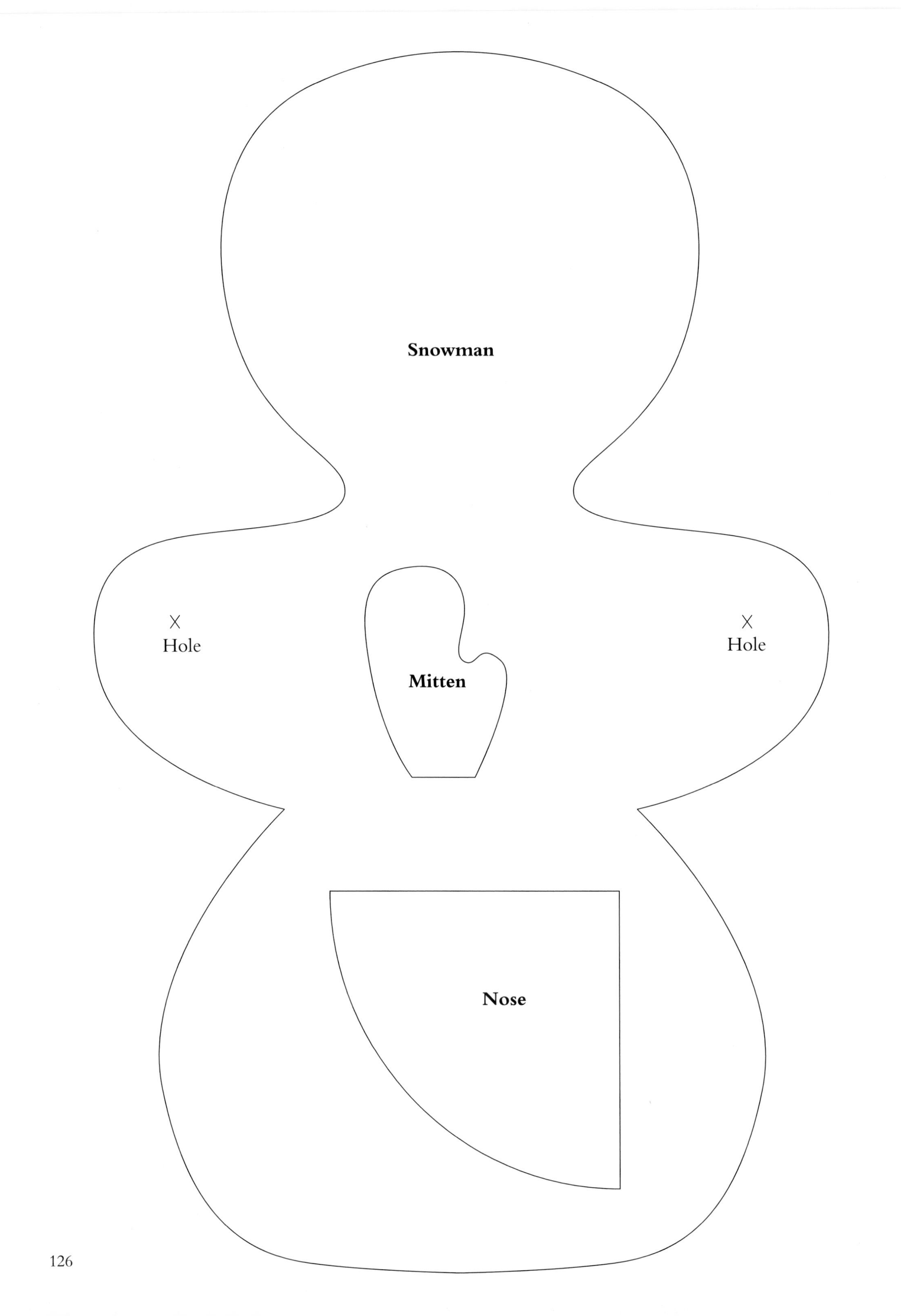
Snowman
X
Hole
Mitten
X
Hole
Nose

Tiny Triangle Trees

Glue together fabric triangles to form festive ornaments for your tree. If desired, attach the ornaments to a length of ribbon or greenery to make a garland for your mantel.

Materials
For each: **Aleene's Fusible Web™**
Print fabric squares: 1 each 2¼", 2½", 3"
Stuffing
Pinking shears
2½" length brown single-fold bias tape
Aleene's Tacky Glue™
8" length gold metallic thread
Assorted trims: sequins, star buttons, ribbon scraps, glitter

Directions for 1 tree

Note: See page 5 for tips on working with fusible web.

1 With wrong sides facing, fold each fabric square in half diagonally to form 1 triangle and finger-press. For each triangle, fuse ¼"-wide strips of web on wrong side of fabric along 2 edges. Stuff each triangle lightly and fuse. Trim fused edges of each triangle with pinking shears (see photo).

2 With wrong sides facing, fuse bias tape layers together. Fold fused bias tape length in half to form loop and finger-press. Referring to photo, glue triangles together to form tree. Glue ends of bias tape to back of tree at bottom for trunk. Fold metallic thread in half to form loop and knot ends. Glue knot to back of tree at top. Let dry. Referring to photo for inspiration, decorate tree with assorted trims as desired.

Designs by Hancock Fabrics

RAG MOP SANTAS

Glue yarn to a wooden ball head to make a mop-head Santa ornament.

Materials

For each: **1¼"-diameter wooden ball**
Aleene's Premium-Coat™ Acrylic Paints: Blush, True Red, Black
Fine-tip paintbrush
⅛"-diameter wooden ball
1 skein off-white yarn
3" square cardboard
Aleene's Designer Tacky Glue™
5" length ¹⁄₁₆"-wide red ribbon
Large-eyed needle
Small stem artificial evergreen
Assorted trims

Directions for 1 ornament

1 Paint 1¼" ball Blush. Let dry. Paint True Red cheeks and Black eyes on ball. Let dry. Paint ⅛" ball True Red. Let dry.

2 For beard, wrap yarn around cardboard square 40 times. Cut 1 (6") length of yarn. At 1 end, slip 6" yarn length under wrapped yarn and knot. Cut wrapped yarn at other end. Repeat to make hair. Glue beard to face with knotted yarn centered between cheeks. Glue hair to top of head. Let dry. Glue red ball to face for nose. Let dry.

3 Thread needle with ribbon. Stitch through yarn at top of head. Remove needle. Double-knot ribbon close to hair. Knot ribbon ends, leaving 2" loop for hanger. Curve evergreen stem into halo, twisting ends together to secure. Glue halo to head. Let dry. Referring to photo, glue assorted trims to ornament as desired. Let dry.

Design by Maria Nerius, SCD

Merry Mirror Image

Make a mirror-image banner using fusible web and holiday print fabrics.

Design by Hancock Fabrics

Materials

For each: **10½" x 36" piece felt**
Aleene's Tacky Glue™
8" x 22" piece print fabric
Aleene's Fusible Web™
2½ yards ½"-wide flat braid or trim
12" length ½"-diameter wooden dowel
Aleene's Premium-Coat™ Acrylic Paint: Holiday Red
Paintbrush
½ yard ribbon or decorative cording

Directions for 1 banner

Note: See page 5 for tips on working with fusible web.

1 Fold felt in half lengthwise. Referring to Diagram, trim 1 short end to make point. Unfold felt. For casing, turn under 1" at other short end of banner and glue. Let dry.

2 Fuse web to wrong side of print fabric. With right sides facing, fold fabric in half lengthwise. Write message on paper side of web, with bottom of writing aligned with fold. Pin layers together along marked lines. Cut out message, adding ¼" all around. *Do not cut along fold.* Unfold message. Center and fuse message on right side of banner (see photo). Glue braid or trim around edge on right side of banner. Let dry.

3 Paint dowel Holiday Red. Let dry. Slip dowel through casing. For hanger, knot 1 end of ribbon or cording at each end of dowel.

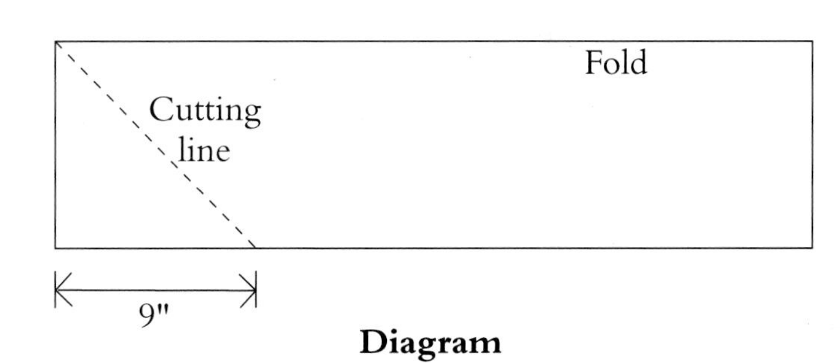

Diagram

Eyelet Angel

Place this lacy angel on your mantel to watch over your family during the holidays.

Materials

Singer sewing machine light bulb #2119
Aleene's Tacky Glue™
¼" flat shader paintbrush
Iridescent glitter
9"-high Styrofoam cone
Blonde curly hair
4" length iridescent teardrop beads
1¾ yards white eyelet flounce
Thread
Gold craft wire
Ribbon: 1 (18") length ¼"-wide red, 3 (12") lengths ⅛"-wide red
1½" iridescent flower shank button

Directions

Note: Use ¼" seam allowance.

1 Brush coat of glue on light bulb. Sprinkle glitter onto wet glue. Let dry. Mix 1 teaspoon of glue with ½ teaspoon of water. Brush glue mixture over glitter to seal. Let dry. For head, push bottom of bulb into tip of cone to form indentation. Remove bulb. Apply glue to bottom of bulb and press into cone. Let dry. Glue hair to bulb. Let dry. For halo, curve teardrop bead length into circle and glue to head. Let dry.

2 With eyelet border along 1 long edge of each piece, cut 1 (10" x 25") piece for dress and 1 (9" x 24") piece for wings. With eyelet border along wrist, transfer pattern to remaining eyelet and cut 2 arms. With right sides facing and edges aligned, fold 10" x 25" eyelet in half widthwise. Stitch short ends of fabric together to form tube. Turn. Run gathering thread along raw edge of tube. Pull thread to gather fabric to fit top of cone. Secure thread. Glue gathered edge of dress to cone. Let dry. Tie ¼"-wide ribbon in bow around gathered area of dress.

3 Turn under ⅛" twice along each short end of 9" x 24" eyelet and stitch for hem. Beginning at 1 (9") end, accordion-fold eyelet with ½"-deep pleats. Twist wire tightly around folded eyelet about 2" from raw edge. Let top of wings unfold. Arrange folds as desired. With top of wings about 3" above head, glue wings to back of angel. Let dry. Tie 1 (12") ribbon length in bow and glue to cover wired area of wings. Let dry.

4 With right sides facing and raw edges aligned, fold 1 arm piece in half along fold line at shoulder. Stitch side raw edges together to form arm, leaving wrist open. Clip seam allowance as needed and turn. Repeat for remaining arm. With shoulder aligned with gathered area of dress, glue each arm in place on angel. Let dry.

5 Glue wrists together at front of angel. Tie remaining 12" ribbon lengths to shank of flower button. Glue button to wrists. Let dry.

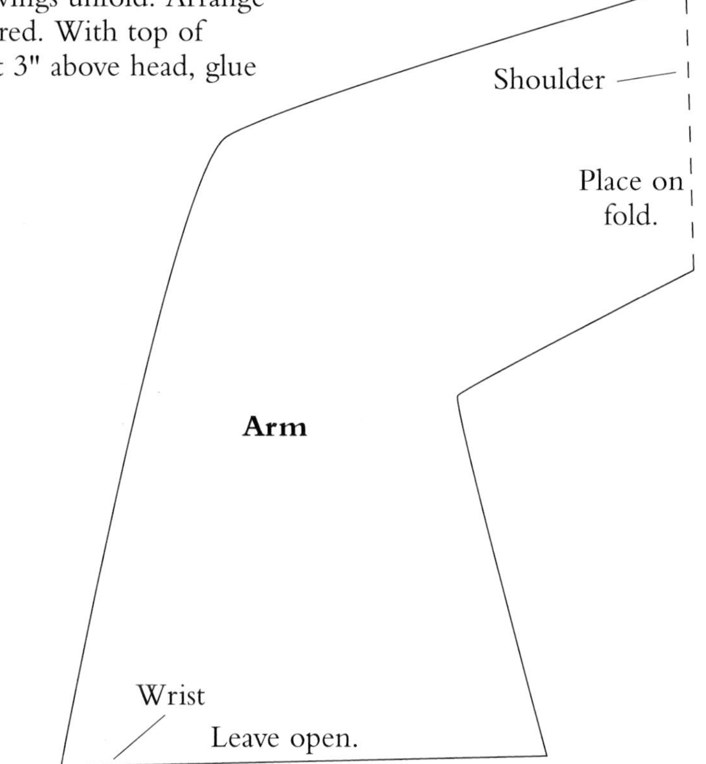

Design by Hancock Fabrics

All That Glitters

Renew old glass or plastic ornaments with dimensional gold foil designs.

Materials
For each: **Glass or plastic ornament**
Aleene's 3-D Foiling Glue™
Aleene's Gold Crafting Foil™

Directions for 1 ornament

Draw design on ornament as desired, using glue. Let dry. (Glue will be opaque and sticky when dry. Glue must be thoroughly dry before foil is applied.) To apply gold foil, lay foil dull side down on top of glue lines. Using finger, gently but firmly press foil onto glue, completely covering glue with foil. Peel away foil paper. If any part of glue is not covered, reapply foil as needed.

Designs by Darsee Lett and Pattie Donham/Hobby Lobby Stores

Design by Charlotte Brown/Beverly Crafts

Americana Accent

Show your patriotic spirit by making and displaying a red-white-and-blue fabric wreath.

Materials
45"-wide fabric: 2 yards each red, white; 1½ yards blue
Pinking shears
14"-diameter straw wreath
Plastic wrap (optional)
Phillips screwdriver
Aleene's Tacky Glue™
White spray paint
25 (¾") wooden stars

Directions

1 Cut fabric into 4" squares, using pinking shears. If desired, wrap wreath with plastic wrap. Position tip of screwdriver in center of 1 fabric square. Gather fabric around screwdriver. Dip fabric tip into glue and poke into wreath. Referring to photo for color placement, repeat to apply remaining fabric squares to wreath until wreath is covered. (*Note:* Approximately ⅔ of wreath is covered with red and white stripes. Remaining ⅓ of wreath is covered with blue.) Let dry.

2 Spray-paint wooden stars. Let dry. Referring to photo, glue stars to blue area of wreath. Let dry.

Pumpkin Breeze Banner

Design by Old America Stores

Hang this durable banner from a tree branch or lamp post and watch the ribbons dance and swirl with the breeze.

Materials

- 9" x 12" Foamies craft foam sheets: 2 orange; 1 each black, green
- Aleene's Leather Glue™
- 10 (1-yard) lengths 1⅜"-wide orange ribbon
- ⅛"-diameter hole punch
- 1 yard string

Directions

1 Transfer patterns to foam sheets and cut 2 pumpkins from orange, 2 eyes and 1 mouth from black, and 2 leaves from green. Glue eyes, mouth, and leaves in place on 1 pumpkin (see photo). Let dry.

2 Glue ½" of 1 end of each of 5 ribbon lengths to wrong side of each pumpkin along bottom edge. Let dry. With wrong sides facing, glue pumpkins together. Let dry. Punch 1 hole in center top of pumpkin (see photo). Thread string through hole and knot ends for hanger.

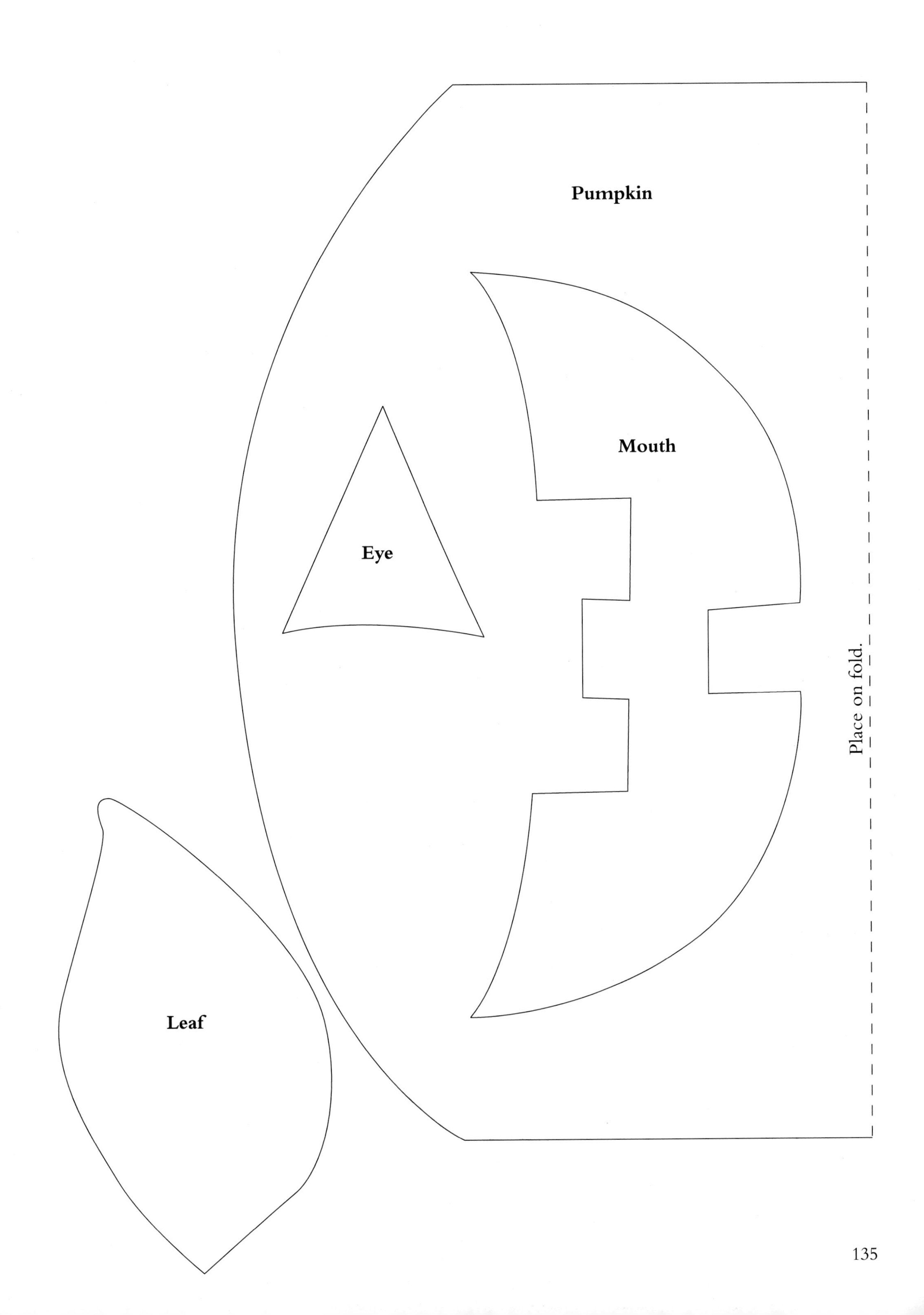
Pumpkin
Mouth
Eye
Leaf
Place on fold.

BOO!

Spooky Shirts

Easy-to-use spray paints let you make these Halloween wearables in a snap.

Materials

2 white T-shirts
Self-adhesive vinyl
Waxed paper
Delta Color Mist™: Emerald Green, Pumpkin, Sunflower Yellow, Black
2½"-high alphabet stencils
Ultra fine-tip permanent black marker

Directions

For pumpkin shirt, transfer patterns to vinyl and cut 10 large and 10 small pumpkins. Transfer pattern to vinyl and cut pieces of grass to fit across hem of shirt front and around bottom of each sleeve. Referring to photo, adhere vinyl cutouts to front and sleeves of 1 shirt. Lay shirt right side up on work surface covered with waxed paper. Spray-paint hem of shirt and bottom of each sleeve Emerald Green. Spray-paint remainder of shirt with Pumpkin and Sunflower Yellow alternately (see photo). Let dry.

Carefully remove vinyl cutouts from shirt. Clean cutouts with paper towel. Adhere cutouts to back of shirt and paint shirt as before. Let dry. Remove cutouts. To spatter-paint pumpkins, lightly spray each pumpkin with Pumpkin, holding bottle about 16" from shirt. Let dry. Lightly spray-paint grass areas with Emerald Green, covering other areas of shirt with waxed paper. Let dry.

For ghost shirt, transfer patterns to vinyl and cut 10 ghosts. Transfer letters to vinyl and cut 1 B, 2 Os, and 1 exclamation point. Referring to photo, adhere vinyl cutouts to front of remaining shirt. Lay shirt right side up on work surface covered with waxed paper. Referring to photo, spray-paint shirt with Pumpkin and Black. Let dry. Carefully remove vinyl cutouts. Spray "Boo!" with Pumpkin. Let dry. Clean cutouts with paper towel. Adhere cutouts to back of shirt and paint shirt as before. Let dry. Remove cutouts.

For each, outline designs and add details with marker.

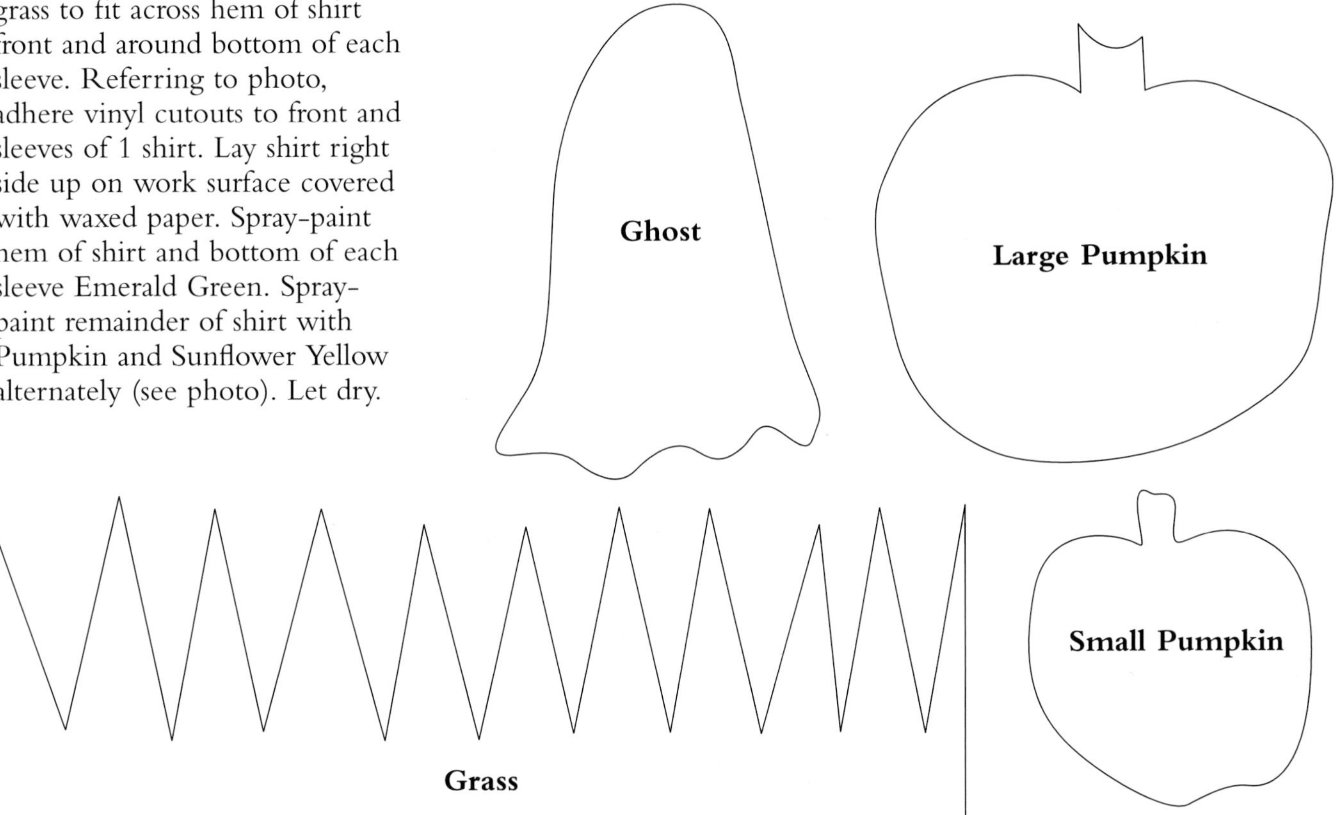

Designs by Joyce Bennett, SCD, CCD, CPD/Delta Technical Coatings

*P*umpkin *D*umplin'

Perch this happy hobgoblin beside your treat bowl to welcome Halloween visitors.

Materials

Styrofoam balls: 1 (3"-diameter), 1 (5"-diameter)
Serrated knife
Batting: 1 (17"-diameter) circle, 1 (8"-diameter) circle
Aleene's Designer Tacky Glue™
Orange-and-white dot fabric: 1 (18"-diameter) circle, 1 (9"-diameter) circle
8" x 12" piece green fabric
Thread
Stuffing
Toothpick
Felt scraps: green, black
9" x 18" piece black Halloween print fabric
Aleene's Fusible Web™
Pinking shears
1 yard ¼"-wide green satin ribbon

Directions

Note: See page 5 for tips on working with fusible web.

Use ¼" seam allowance for stitching.

1 For body, cut ¼"-thick slice from top and bottom of 5" foam ball, using serrated knife. Wrap and glue 17" batting circle around foam ball, trimming excess batting to leave flat areas uncovered. Center and place batting-covered ball on wrong side of 18" fabric circle. Gather fabric around ball, poking fabric edges into flat area at top of ball, using knife.

2 Transfer patterns to green fabric and cut 2 arms and 2 legs. Reverse patterns and cut 2 more arms and 2 more legs from green. With right sides facing and raw edges aligned, stitch 2 arms together, leaving straight edge open. Turn. Stuff lightly. Turn under ¼" around open end and glue opening closed. Repeat for remaining arm and both legs. Poke straight end of 1 arm into top of body at each side, using knife. Glue straight end of each leg to bottom of body in sitting position (see photo). Let dry.

3 Cut ¼"-thick slice from bottom of 3" foam ball. Wrap and glue 8" batting circle around ball, trimming excess batting to leave flat area uncovered. Center and place batting-covered ball on wrong side of 9" fabric circle. Gather fabric around ball, poking fabric edges into flat area at bottom of ball, using knife. Dip 1 end of toothpick into glue. Push toothpick into bottom of head. Dip free end of toothpick into glue and push into top of body. Let dry.

Design by Betty Ann Lasley/Dow Chemical Co.

4 Transfer patterns to felt and cut 1 leaf from green, and 3 triangles and 1 mouth from black. Cut 1 (1" x 1½") piece from remaining green felt. For stem, roll 1" x 1½" green felt piece jellyroll fashion, gluing end to secure. Glue leaf and stem to top of head. Glue facial features on face. Let dry.

5 For cape, fuse ½"-wide strip of web along 1 (18") edge of Halloween print fabric. Turn under 2" along this edge and fuse for casing. Trim remaining edges of fabric with pinking shears, rounding bottom corners. Thread ribbon through casing. Wrap cape around pumpkin doll and tie ribbon in bow.

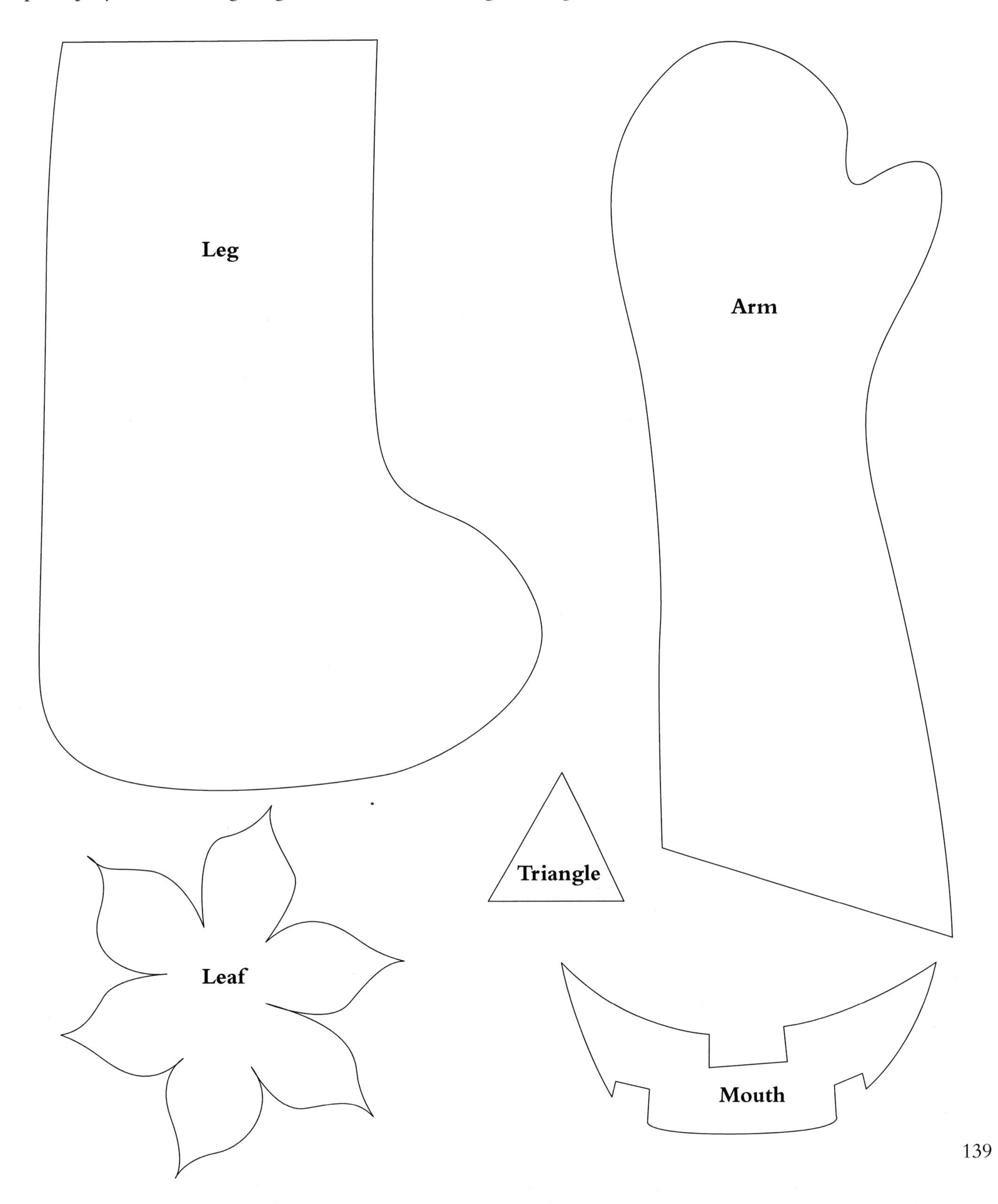

TO:
FROM:
I "carrot" for you bunches

Hoppy Easter Bag

Fuse fabric shapes onto a brown sack for a whimsical Easter gift presentation.

Materials

Print fabric scraps: pink, light green
Aleene's Fusible Web™
10"-tall brown gift sack
Tissue paper
Permanent black markers: fine-tip, wide-tip
Natural raffia
Aleene's Tacky Glue™
Gift tag

Directions

Note: See page 5 for tips on working with fusible web.

1 Fuse web onto wrong side of fabric scraps. Transfer pattern to web and cut 3 carrots from pink and 3 tops from light green. Referring to photo for placement, arrange fabric cutouts on bag front. Carefully lay 1 piece of tissue paper over bag front. Fuse cutouts to bag. Discard tissue paper.

2 Outline fabric cutouts and add details with fine-tip marker. Cut 12" lengths of raffia. Tie raffia into 3 bows. Glue 1 bow to each carrot. Write message on bag below carrots with wide-tip marker (see photo). Tie gift tag onto handle of bag.

Top

Carrot

Design by Sharon Rodriguez/Just Bag It!

Bunny Pins

Accessorize your Easter outfit with a well-dressed bunny.

Materials
***For each:* Aleene's Opake Shrink-It™ Plastic**
Fine-grade sandpaper
Fine-tip permanent black marker
Colored pencils: gray, white, pink
Aleene's Baking Board or nonstick cookie sheet, sprinkled with baby powder
Fabric scraps
Thread to match fabric
Aleene's Designer Tacky Glue™
Embroidery floss to match fabric
Clothespin
Pin back

Directions for 1 bunny

1 Sand 1 side of Shrink-It so that markings will adhere. Be sure to thoroughly sand entire surface both vertically and horizontally. Transfer patterns to unsanded side of Shrink-It, using marker. **For woman bunny,** cut 1 bunny and 1 arms, cutting just inside marked line. **For man bunny,** cut 1 bunny, 1 arms, 1 hat, and 1 basket, cutting just inside marked line. **For each,** use colored pencils on sanded side of Shrink-It to color each piece (see photo). Draw facial features and details with marker.

2 Preheat toaster oven or conventional oven to 275° to 300°. Place each design on room-temperature baking board and bake in oven. Edges should begin to curl within 25 seconds; if not, increase temperature slightly. If edges begin to curl as soon as design is put in oven, reduce temperature. After about 1 minute, design will lie flat. Remove from oven. Let cool.

3 **For woman bunny,** cut 1 (1¾" x 3") piece of fabric for dress. Fringe 1 (3") edge of fabric. Run gathering thread along remaining 3" edge of fabric. Gather fabric around bunny's neck and secure thread. Overlap ends of fabric at back of bunny and glue. Glue arms to back of bunny. Use clothespin to hold arms in place until glue is dry.

For man bunny, using bunny as guide, cut fabric scraps for shirt and pants. Using arms as guide, cut fabric scraps for shirt sleeves. Glue arms to back of bunny. Use clothespin to hold arms in place until glue is dry. Referring to photo, glue fabric pieces in place on front of bunny. Glue hat and basket in place on bunny. Let dry.

4 **For each,** tie small bow with embroidery floss and glue to bunny's neck. Let dry. Center and glue pin back to back of bunny. Glue 1 fabric scrap over pin back for stability. Let dry.

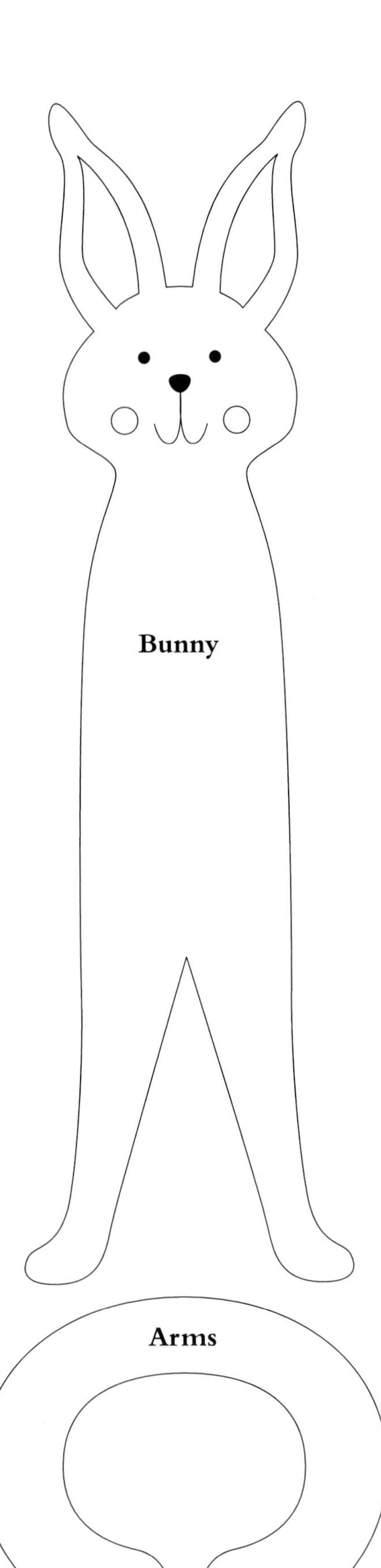

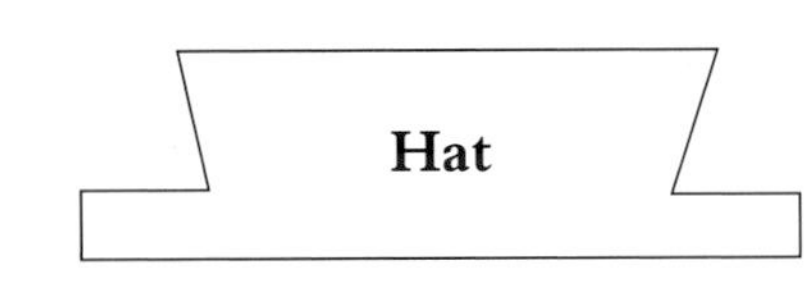

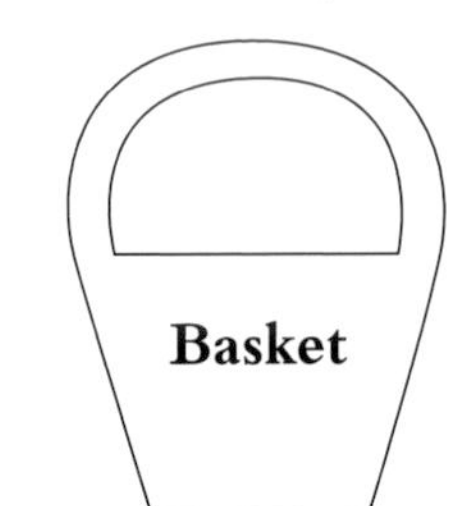

Index

Designs by Heidi Borchers.
SCD/Aleene's